WHY BEING AN INTROVERT IS A SUPERPOWER

HACKNEY AND JONES

Copyright © 2021 by Hackney And Jones

All rights reserved.

No part of this book may be reproduced in any form or by any electronic or mechanical means, including information storage and retrieval systems, without written permission from the author, except for the use of brief quotations in a book review.

Claim Your Freebie NOW!

Get Good At Problem Solving

Want to know the secret behind getting good at problem solving? Everyone seems to be able to do it, but you're stuck in the pile of endless to-do lists with little progress.

Ok, so how do I get my FREE book?

EASY! See the next page

Claim Your Freebie NOW

Instructions:

1. Open the camera or the QR reader application on your smartphone.
2. Point your camera at the QR code to scan the QR code.
3. A notification will pop-up on screen.
4. Click on the notification to open the website link

Claim Your Freebie NOW

Instruction:

1. Open the camera / scanner QR Reader application on your smartphone.
2. Point your camera at the QR code to scan the QR code.
3. A notification will pop-up on-screen.
4. Click on the notification to open the website.

SCAN ME

Contents

Introduction	ix
1. Understanding Introversion	1
2. Are You An Introvert?	3
3. Considering Shyness	11
4. Getting In Touch With Sensitivity	18
5. How Introverts And Extroverts Differ	25
6. Am I An Introvert?	28
7. The Different Faces Of Introversion	30
8. Facts About Introverts	32
9. Determining What Makes You An Introvert	36
10. When Temporarily Playing The Extrovert Can Work To Your Advantage	42
11. Can You Become A Real Extrovert?	48
12. Introverts In The Workplace	52
13. Jobs That Appeal To Introverts And Extroverts	65
14. Introvert With Leadership Skills	69
15. Anticipating The Difficulties Of Leading As An Introvert	72
16. Reinforcing Effectively	77
17. Boosting Your Emotional Intelligence	82
18. Raising Your Own Emotional Intelligence	84
19. Introverts And Public Speaking	88
20. Grabbing Your Audience: How To Win Them Over	105
21. Dating Advice For Introverts	117
22. What If Your Child Is An Introvert	137
Afterword	147
Feedback	149

Introduction

Introverts can be found at the top of every sector and industry, from entrepreneurs like Bill Gates to fashion designers like Eileen Fisher, athletes like Michael Jordan, and film directors like Ang Lee. Despite their introversion, these celebrities have succeeded. Instead, their introverted qualities have aided them in their success. You, too, are an introvert with such qualities.

Unfortunately, not every workplace is designed to promote the success of all employees. Modern workplaces cater to gregarious extroverts with noisy open-plan offices, brainstorming meetings, and required (fun!) socialising with team-building activities and holiday parties.

You have the power of quietness, the edge of reflection, and the ability to look before leaping. Despite the advantages of being an introvert, you can find yourself in conflict with a society that views extroversion as the ideal disposition. You might feel out of place and discriminate against—and you might even be the one doing the discriminating! You may be misunderstood, criticised, and undervalued. The noise, activity, and stress of ordinary life may also overwhelm you.

This book will give you a thorough set of skills for understanding and working with your introversion. You'll discover your distinct introvert characteristics and establish self-care skills to deal with the pressures you confront in the real world. These mindfulness-based tactics can assist you in maximising your introvert skills and finding balance within and outside of yourself in an extrovert-dominated culture. Using mindfulness to optimise your introverted assets can help you thrive one moment at a time. Information is powerful, and it has the potential to lead to self-acceptance. You don't have to feel bad about being an introvert any longer. You can become aware of your abilities. Mindfulness practice can also assist you in realising your full human potential.

Why are we writing this book?

This book is written for anyone who feels challenged, overwhelmed, or stressed by the responsibilities of living in an extrovert-dominated culture. These stresses can be found at home with your spouse and children, at work, or in your larger social network. It will also benefit extroverts who are stressed by the fast-paced, never-ending speed of life and desire to hone their introverted tendencies. Everyone is a mix of introverts and extroverts; no one is completely one or the other. However, depending on the important defining qualities, it is still common to refer to people as "introverts" or "extroverts."

We'll give you a set of potent memory-enhancing mindsets and abilities in this short, easy-to-read book, allowing you to take control of your learning and your life. You'll learn about a variety of wonderful approaches for rapid learning and memory improvement, both old and new, that have been modelled after the world's top minds in the field. The strategy controls your mind, which is only feasible with a solid foundation in memory.

1

Understanding Introversion

DOES any of the following describe you? You'd rather read a book than attending a dinner gathering. You adore your friends, but you cherish your alone moments. You'd rather eat nails than go to a business team-building activity.

This means you're an introvert if any of these apply to you. Furthermore, this means your extroverted friends have no idea who you are.

Yes, these people adore you. They don't understand, though, why noisy team meetings and brainstorming sessions tire you. They're baffled as to why you prefer hiking or fiddling in your kitchen to karaoke at a crowded bar. Above all, most of them believe they can (and should) change your attitude.

Here's the truth: If you're introverted, you're probably hard-wired to be that way. In a world that is mostly tailored toward extroverts, you can be tremendously successful — and that is exactly what this book is about. But deep down inside, you'll always be an introvert.

Although there is nothing wrong with being an introvert, living in an extrovert-dominated world can make you doubt your abilities as one. Trying to keep up with the extroverted speed of life may throw you off balance. You may have forgotten what silence, solitude, and depth means to you. This book will assist you in maximising your introvert qualities while also protecting you from the extrovert culture. You might think of this workbook as a how-to guide for surviving in today's digitally dominated culture. Introverts can communicate safely and selectively on social media; you can participate when and where you want. However, the same technology increases accessibility and expectations that you should be on, available, and responsive at all times. Even if you can use social media whenever you want, there are still expectations that you share. It's also difficult to retain a sense of calm in these settings. Extroverts may like the stimulating abundance of information available on the Internet, but introverts may find it overwhelming.

Introverts are not extroverts who have failed. It's past time for this culture to recognise introverts' quiet strengths. The methods in this book will empower you to be who you are without regret if you have been disempowered.

2

Are You An Introvert?

YOU'RE AN INTROVERT, according to your best friend. Your mother describes you as sensitive, and your father describes you as shy.

So, who is correct and who is incorrect? The answer isn't as straightforward as you may assume. Shyness, sensitivity, and introversion all have separate meanings, yet they often overlap.

You may, for example, exhibit many features of an introvert, some of those of a shy person, and a few of those of a sensitive individual. It's the fact that people don't easily fit into cookie-cutter shapes that makes them so intriguing. Whether you're a straight-laced innie, a bashful person, or a sensitive soul, there's something for you in this book.

EXPLORING **the introvert continuum**

The first thing to understand about introversion is that nearly no one is completely introverted. (Well, hermits come close, but there aren't many of them.) In actuality, everyone falls somewhere between extroversion and introversion, with the ambiverts occupying a medium ground.

You may also discover that you are introverted in certain aspects but not in others.

So, when examining your personality, don't think "all or nothing." Instead, recognise that every innie contains a small amount of extrovert, and every outie has a small introvert. When it comes to introversion and extroversion, there are many shades of grey.

Do you think you're an introvert? Take the quiz to find out.

To find out if you're an innie, you can take various "official" exams. You might even come across one of these tests at work, as many organisations employ them. However, by taking the following simple little test, you may get a rough indication of whether you're introverted or extroverted. It's pretty accurate, even if it's not scientific! To receive the best results, make sure you answer all of the questions.

INFORMAL INNIE/OUTIE Test

Consider what is normally true for you when you answer these questions.

1. Which do you like to do at work?
   A. I prefer to work on my own.
   B. I prefer to work as part of a group.

2. How do you feel after being at a party with your buddies for two and a half hours?
   A. I'm in a state of exhaustion.
   B. I have a lot of energy.

. . .

3. What do you do if you're giving a brief speech on a topic you know a lot about and the audience is excitedly responding?

A. Focusing on my topic keeps me energised.

B. I concentrate on my subject, but I also benefit from the pleasant energy generated by my audience.

4. How do you deal with personal issues?

A. Even if it causes delays, I like to think things out first and develop a good plan.

B. I usually confide in others about my difficulties, and I may begin taking action before I have a complete plan in mind.

5. What do you usually do in a meeting?

A. I sit silently and only speak when I am sure I have a good idea.

B. I speak up on any subject that interests me.

6. What did you do when you were a kid and didn't grasp something the teacher said?

A. I kept my puzzlement to myself and attempted to solve it later on my own.

B. I'd be perplexed or ask a question.

7. Which of the following statements most accurately describes you?

A. I enjoy a small number of intimate friendships, and I've never felt compelled to have a large number of people who "like" me.

B. I like having a large group of friends.

. . .

8. What is your preferred method of acquiring new knowledge?
  A. I adore spending hours reading in bookshops or on the Internet.
  B. I like attending lectures or seminars where I can mingle with other people while learning from experts.

9. How long can you keep focused when working on a difficult task?
  A. I can labour for hours and not notice the passage of time.
  B. I require "people" breaks regularly.

10. What should you do if you can't solve a problem?
  A. I tend to think about it a lot.
  B. I'm good at moving on and letting go.

11. What are your thoughts on spending time alone or with your family at home?
  A. It gives me a sense of utter fulfilment.
  B. I enjoy my home life, but if I don't have any outside activities, I become restless or depressed.

12. Which of the following statements best describes you?
  A. I'm a reserved person.
  B. I'm a friendly person.

13. What gives you a boost of energy?
  A. After mulling over some new ideas in my head or on paper, I feel energised.

B. After being around people, I notice a boost in my energy.

14. Which of the following best describes how you'll react in a crowded, high-pressure meeting?
   A. Mentally, I'll probably shut down and want to flee.
   B. I'll be there in the heart of it — and I'll be energised by the atmosphere.

15. What are you most likely to do if a distant relative calls?
   A. I'll leave it on the answering machine so I can figure out what she wants before calling her.
   B. I'm going to pick up the phone.

16. What are your major aims when you shop for clothes, shoes, or accessories?
   A. I'm looking for anything that will make me feel at ease and allow me to blend in.
   B. I try to think of something that will make people look at me and say, "Wow!"

17. Which of the following represents you best?
   A. I pick a few things and get into them thoroughly.
   B. I attempt a lot of new activities.

18. When you meet new individuals, do you share a lot of personal information with them?
   A. No. I open up to just close friends.
   B. Yes, because it's an excellent method to get to know them.

19. How comfortable are you with small conversations at parties?
  A. I hate it.
  B. I enjoy it.

20. Can you multi-task easily?
  A. No. I prefer to tackle one job at a time and give it all my concentration.
  B. Sure, no issue!

21. How would you react if your company paid for you to participate in a two-day team-building exercise?
  A. I'd think to myself, "Is there any way out of this?"
  B. I believe, "Oh, my goodness! But for only two days?"

AS YOU PROBABLY SUSPECTED, introverts often answer "A" to these questions, whereas extroverts say "B." So, if you answered "A" the majority of the time, you're probably the real deal when it comes to introversion.

And, because introverts enjoy serious thought, here's another technique you could enjoy.

THE INNIE/OUTIE Interests Questionnaire

Take a few minutes to contemplate each of the following questions:

1. As a 5-year-old, what were your favourite pastimes? What would you do if you were ten years old? As an adolescent?

Consider the hobbies that you enjoy the most, rather than what your parents intended you to do.

2. When you were a kid, what activities did you wish you could do?

3. What are your current favourite pastimes?

4. What would your favourite pastimes be if you had the time and money to do whatever you wanted?

5. How would you spend a week without watching TV, using your computer, or using your smartphone or other electronic devices?

6. When your parents, grandparents, aunts, and uncles were adults (especially those who were retired and could do whatever they wanted), what were their interests? What are your siblings' interests, if you have any?

AS YOU EVALUATE YOUR RESPONSES, you'll likely discover patterns, such as the following:

Most introverts reveal their colours early in childhood by favouring innie pastimes, such as reading or drawing. So, if you've always like innie activities, you're probably an introvert.

When asked the question, "What would you do if you were rich and could do anything?" most introverted adults instantly choose an innie interest. "I'd purchase a farm out in the middle of nowhere and raise chickens," one of my acquaintances responded quickly.

By evaluating what their relatives loved to achieve best, most people can track their introvert or extrovert genes back at least a few generations.

You should have a fair idea of where you fall on the innie/outie spectrum after taking the informal innie/outie test and filling out the interests questionnaire. But there are two more attributes to consider if you want to know yourself genuinely: shyness and sensitivity.

3

Considering Shyness

MANY PEOPLE mistakenly believe that introversion and shyness are the same things, yet they are not. In fact, as this section shows, many extroverts are shy, whereas many introverts aren't.

You can use the simple test provided in this section to determine whether or not you are shy. And if you find yourself to be shy, you'll appreciate these ideas for prospering in social circumstances.

IDENTIFYING the difference between shyness and introversion

What's the difference between shyness and introversion? Introverts prefer being alone over being in a crowd, yet they are completely comfortable in social settings. On the other hand, Shy people desire to interact with others, but their nervousness prevents them from doing so. Here are two examples to demonstrate the difference:

Alice receives an invitation to her friend Kate's holiday party. She'd rather watch It's a Wonderful Life on the couch with her husband, but she knows Kate wants her to show up, so she does. Alice meets some interesting individuals at the party and has a fantastic time conversing with them, but after two hours, she informs her husband that it's time to go home.

Jack is also invited to the same holiday gathering. He's looking forward to meeting Kate since he believes she's a lot of fun and wants to learn more about her. But he's nervous and uncomfortable during the gathering. He blushes beet-red as Kate replies, "You look handsome tonight." Other people try to strike up a conversation with him, but he is completely speechless. He mentally kicks himself for being so awkward when he gets home.

Alice, the first partygoer, is an introvert who isn't afraid to speak up. She isn't a natural mingler, but when she attends a social gathering, she starts conversations comfortably and frequently has a good time (as long as she can escape after a few hours). If you questioned Kate's other guests about her, they'd most likely respond, "Alice?" She's a fascinating woman. I had a lot of fun talking to her."

What about Jack now? He's shy, but not shy in the sense that he's not introverted. He likes to mingle, but when he meets new people, he feels nervous. He's afraid they'll have a poor impression of him, making it difficult for him to speak up. "Alex is a wonderful guy, but he sure is quiet, isn't he?" Kate's visitors would undoubtedly reply if you questioned them about him.

Jack displays the typical indications of shyness. He isn't always shy, though, like most shy people. He can easily converse with anyone at work, where he is confident and well-liked. He can also be the life of the party during family gatherings! However, during a job interview, a party, or a date, he feels self-conscious, gets butterflies in his stomach, stammers, and sweats his palms.

TAKING THE TEST: Are you shy?

If you're wondering how shy you are, here's a fast test to help you figure it out. This isn't a scientific test, but it's entertaining and fairly accurate. Simply select "A" or "B" for each question.

1. When you're socialising with somebody you don't know well, do you get nervous or tongue-tied?
A. Yes
B. No

2. Do you have a strong fear of being rejected by others in social situations?
A. Yes
B. No

3. Do you find yourself replaying social occasions in your mind, feeling embarrassed or ashamed of something you said or did?
A. Yes
B. No

4. Do you ever feel lonely and wish you could spend more time socialising with others?
A. Yes
B. No

5. Do you allow others to take advantage of you because you're afraid of standing out or gaining attention?
A. Yes
B. No

6. Do you find it difficult to share your feelings with others?
   A. Yes
   B. No

7. Do you instantly assume it's your fault if someone rejects you?
   A. Yes
   B. No

8. Do you spend a lot of time trying to figure out how to avoid getting rejected or how to make others like you?
   A. Yes
   B. No

PEOPLE WHO AREN'T SHY USUALLY ANSWER "B" to these questions, while those who are shy usually answer "A." As a result, the more "A" answers you have, the shyer you are.

DEALING with shyness

If you're shy and content with it, that's great! Shyness isn't a problem if it doesn't get in the way of your life. "Shyness is not a disability or disease to be 'overcome,'" says famous (and shy) humorist Garrison Keillor. "It's just the way we're built. And we're secretly proud of it in our quiet way."

And shy people should be proud of themselves! Some of the world's most well-known writers, painters, scientists, teachers, doctors, nurses, and, surprisingly, entertainers are among them. (Extrovert Barbra Streisand is notoriously shy.) Shy people are frequently high achievers who are content with themselves as they are.

But what if you're not content with your shyness? Extreme shyness might hold you back as a student by making it difficult for you to speak up in class. It can be challenging to be assertive in meetings if you're attempting to advance your career. Being shy might also make it difficult to make connections with the individuals you want to meet.

There's good news if you discover that shyness is a problem for you. Most experts feel that if you want to, you can overcome your shyness — or at the very least figure out how to work around it.

Here are some tricks to try if you think your shyness is causing you problems:

- Visualise yourself having a good time before going to a party or a meeting. Consider how easy it is for you to make eye contact with others, tell them about yourself or your ideas, and appreciate their attention.
- Get over your fear of being rejected. Here's a basic exercise to get you started. Go up to at least five strangers in a mall or grocery shop and ask a question, such as "What time is it?" or "Can you tell me where the toy store is?" Some people will most likely be pleasant, while others will be brusque or even ignore you. With practice, you'll notice that your nervousness lessens regardless of how people reply.
- Deep breathing techniques should be practised. The five-two-five approach is a nice example. Slowly inhale to the count of five, using your diaphragm to breathe deeply (so the air pushes your tummy outward). Hold your breath for two counts, then gently exhale for five counts. This technique can help you feel less anxious in social situations right away.
- Consider attending a local or online shyness

support group. People who are in the same boat as you can provide support and advice. Also, seeing how brilliant, witty, and intriguing other shy people are when they're comfortable will help you realise that you're pretty cool too.

If your shyness is crippling you, counselling may be a viable solution.

There's a big difference between typical, healthy shyness and significant illnesses when it comes to shyness.

Shyness is a perfectly natural personality feature. Almost everyone is shy at some point in their lives. Some people, on the other hand, go far beyond shyness. They have a social anxiety disorder or avoidant personality disorder, for example.

SOCIAL ANXIETY DISORDER

Some folks are truly terrified of being around other people. This is known as social anxiety disorder, and it is extremely common. It's the third most frequent psychiatric condition! So, if you're experiencing this issue, know that you're not alone. Around 15 million people in the United States are in the same boat as you.

Some people with social anxiety disorder have problems just in specific contexts, such as speaking up at business meetings. (This condition is known as a restricted social anxiety disorder.) Others suffer from a generalised social anxiety disorder, which causes them to panic in any circumstance that requires them to interact with others.

A quick heartbeat, sweaty hands, dizziness, or nausea are all symptoms of social anxiety disorder. Some people feel dizzy or have full-fledged panic attacks. It's not enjoyable. And if you suffer from social anxiety, it can have a significant impact on your social life as well as your profession.

Fortunately, this is a curable condition. Although most doctors will prescribe medicine to treat it, you can also try cognitive behavioural therapy (CBT). CBT assists you in identifying and replacing self-defeating ideas and behaviours with more productive thoughts and behaviours. Group CBT is particularly beneficial since it allows you to confront your concerns in the company of others who understand how you feel.

Avoidant personality disorder

An avoidant personality disorder is a more serious problem. You're self-conscious, afraid of rejection, and obsessed with your own perceived flaws if you have this condition. Poor self-esteem and feelings of inadequacy plague you, and even the mildest criticism seems like a knife through your heart. As a result, you become estranged from others. Because of your symptoms, you may find it difficult to hold a workshop, and you may grow terrified of being in public places, such as shopping malls, or even leaving the house (a condition called agoraphobia). Medications, CBT, and other methods, such as social skills training, can be used to treat avoidant personality disorder or agoraphobia.

Getting help

If you think you could have a social anxiety disorder, avoidant personality disorder, or agoraphobia, seek help right away. Treatment requires time and effort, but it has the potential to improve your life.

The function of perfectionism should be addressed in any therapy for these diseases. People who suffer from these issues frequently create unrealistic expectations for themselves and others. As a result, they are too critical of themselves and everyone around them. People often need to forgive themselves and their loved ones to make true progress in therapy, and they must accept that no one is perfect. (Imagine how dull life would be if we were all like that!)

4

Getting In Touch With Sensitivity

INTROVERTS ARE FREQUENTLY REFERRED to as "sensitive souls." But, like shyness, sensitivity is a unique personality trait that can — but does not always — coexist with introversion. In this section, let's see what sensitivity is, give you a test to check whether you're sensitive, and discuss how to cope as a sensitive person in a world that isn't so sensitive.

IDENTIFYING the difference between sensitivity and introversion

Do bright lights, strong odours, and crowds ever make you feel overwhelmed? Do you become hot or chilly more easily than other individuals when a dog barks? Do you become anxious when a lot is going on or feel compelled to "hide-away" in a darkened room?

If this is the case, you may be more sensitive than others. Though your senses may be on high alert — but also sensitive to subtleties in discussions, emotional tension in a room, and other people's anguish and sadness. Less sensitive people's slings and arrows can deeply harm you, and as a result, you may be hesitant to expose yourself to social situations.

As a result, extremely sensitive persons are sometimes mislabeled as introverts. But there's a distinction:

Introverts prefer isolation over groups because their inner world energises them, and too much contact with other people weakens them.

Whether they're at a busy party, watching a loud movie, or travelling in traffic, sensitive folks can be entirely overwhelmed by the outside world.

It's also worth noting that innies aren't the only ones that are hypersensitive. Extroverts make about 30% of very sensitive persons, according to a study. In general, 15 to 20% of persons are likely to be very sensitive. Sensitivity appears to be a genetic feature; therefore, you were born with it if you're hypersensitive.

TAKING THE TEST: Are you highly sensitive?

Here's another fast test to see if you're a highly sensitive person. It's not scientific, but it's entertaining and can help you figure out how sensitive you are.

1. When you're feeling overwhelmed, do you ever feel the desire to "hide away" in your bedroom or another quiet location?
A. Yes.
B. No.

2. How do you react to a lot of activity, loud noises, and bright lights?
A. I'm feeling stressed and overwhelmed.
B. I love the excitement.

3. Are specific fabrics or tags on your garments uncomfortable to you?
   A. Yes.
   B. No.

4. Do particular odours, such as perfumes elicit strong reactions in you?
   A. Yes.
   B. No.

5. How do you deal with discomfort?
   A. I'm acutely aware of it.
   B. I believe I react in a very normal manner.

6. Are you easily influenced by other people's emotions?
   A. Of course. It irritates me much when someone is furious.
   B. I'm aware of other people's moods, but I don't respond inappropriately.

7. Are you an opportunity to take?
   A. Yes.
   B. No.

8. Are you very conscientious to the point of being obnoxious?
   A. Yes. I fret over even small failures.
   B. No. I try to do a good job, but I don't sweat small mistakes.

. . .

9. Do you think you're more conscientious than the average person?
   A. Yes, and it irritates me when others aren't as conscientious as I am.
   B. No, I think I'm about average in terms of conscientiousness.

10. How do you deal with life's changes?
   A. I become really stressed and may have a nervous breakdown.
   B. I'm a little freaked out, but I'm a good change manager.

11. Do you have a greater sense of seeing small details in your surroundings than other people?
   A. Yes.
   B. No.

12. Do global issues or catastrophes touch you more than they appear to affect others?
   A. Yes.
   B. No.

DID YOU GET MORE "A" responses than "B" responses? If that's the case, you're probably sensitive.

MANAGING sensitive issues

You're watchful, caring, and conscientious if you're sensitive — all positive qualities! A sensitive person's ability to notice nuances and details can be handy in a lot of career fields, from interior design ("that paint colour is just a little off") to psychology ("she says she's fine, but her body language tells us she's worried"). If you're highly sensitive, you're likely to be a deeper thinker with a strong spiritual side. Furthermore, you are more likely than your nonsensitive friends to enjoy the beauty of art and music.

On the other hand, if you're hypersensitive, daily life can be difficult. When things grow hectic, you're more likely to break apart than other people. You're more likely to cry, and you're more likely to feel guilty or ashamed. You have a harder time jumping into new situations, which is why people often mistake you for being shy or introverted. And you might be more sensitive to things like caffeine, sirens, or the pain of vaccination than other people.

Being very sensitive may make it more difficult for you to cope socially or at work for these reasons. If that's the case, don't worry: By performing the following, you can develop more control over your physical and emotional reactions to the world:

- Daily, practice attentive meditation and deep breathing techniques.
- If your office offers a flexi-time policy, try arriving a little earlier than the rest of the staff so you can enjoy some peace before the rest of the gang arrives. To help you survive in a noisy job, use earplugs or headphones.
- Aromatherapy or a long bath can help you relax at home if you're feeling worried. Yoga and Tai Chi are also excellent stress relievers for many sensitive persons.
- Identify the situations that cause you to lose control. Many highly sensitive persons have strong reactions to hunger, so try to eat regularly. If caffeine has a strong effect on you, cut down on coffee, tea, and even chocolate.
- Sleep regularly. If you're having difficulties sleeping, try rubbing a drop of lavender oil on your

bedpost or using a "white noise" machine to drown out traffic noises or barking dogs. (Avoid watching upsetting or loud movies or news shows soon before bedtime.)

MEDITATING your stress away

Mindful meditation is one of the most effective strategies to de-stress if you're hypersensitive. The simplest remedies are often the most effective, and this stress-relieving strategy is no exception. Recent research of 47 highly sensitive people found that practising mindful meditation for eight weeks significantly reduced their stress and social anxiety. In addition, their levels of self-acceptance improved.

Mindful meditation is simple to conduct, though it does require some effort and patience to master. Here's how it's done:

1. Find a peaceful, secluded location, either indoors or outside. Sit in a chair, on the floor, or the ground.

2. Close your eyes and inhale and exhale slowly through your nose. Concentrate on your breathing and how air enters and exits your body. You might wish to try the five-two-five breathing strategy. You might also find it simpler to concentrate on a nonsensical word, known as a mantra, a mental image, such as a candle, or a physical area, such as the back of your hand.

3. Pay attention to how your body feels. (Do you feel hot or cold? Are your arms stiff or relaxed?) Also, pay attention to what's going on around you. (Is it lightly raining outside? Is it possible to hear birds chirping or automobiles passing by?)

. . .

4. Let your feelings and thoughts flow freely without judging them. Simply notice the thought or feeling when you find you've stopped focusing on your breathing instead of thinking about something. Then let it go and return your attention to your breathing.

WHEN YOU FIRST START MEDITATING, you may find it difficult to let go of your concerns and anxiety. However, the more you practice, the easier it will get to enter "the zone." You'll feel calm and relaxed as a result, and this feeling will likely remain long after your session is over.

What is the impact of mindful meditation? According to research, it can change the structure of your brain! According to a new study, merely eight weeks of meditation boosted grey matter density in multiple brain regions, including the left hippocampus, which is important in learning, memory, and emotional control.

5

How Introverts And Extroverts Differ

Have you ever wondered why your outgoing friends think and act in such a different way than you? In this section, you'll see why, as well as look at a range of behaviours that separate innies from outies.

The biggest difference between introverts and extroverts

The first thing to understand about introverts and extroverts is how they recharge their batteries.

Being in the middle of a crowd of people excites extroverts. They can converse for hours and still feel energised and rejuvenated. As a result, they surround themselves with friends and family, and they are eager to meet new people and participate in new activities. Walking into a room full of strangers is like taking a shot of a high-caffeine energy drink for them.

If you're an introvert, you'll find this conduct difficult to comprehend. It's not that you despise them. In reality, you genuinely appreciate them; nevertheless, you do so in moderation. You enjoy having lunch with a good buddy or spending the weekend with close family members. Making endless small conversation at a party full of strangers, on the other hand, does not energise you. In reality, it has the opposite effect: it tires you, and you can't wait to recharge your batteries with a quiet walk, a family dinner, or a nice book.

OTHER WAYS INTROVERTS are different from extroverts

Introverts and extroverts respond to the world differently because introverts gaze inward and extroverts look outward. Here are some of the ways you differ from your extroverted peers if you're an introvert:

- Outies prefer to say anything that comes to mind, whereas you deliberate before you speak.
- You prefer to focus intensely on a few things, whereas extroverts want to dabble in a variety of activities.
- Extroverts like phone calls and face-to-face encounters, while you probably prefer texting or e-mailing individuals.
- Multitasking may be unpleasant for you, but extroverts are usually rather adept at it.
- You're probably more cautious than an extrovert when it comes to taking chances.
- Rather than a large number of casual acquaintances, you have a few close friendships.
- You prefer to wear colours that blend in rather than stand out, and you act in ways that assist you to do so.
- Introverts are often blamed for various behaviours, but some of these are the result of two other personality traits: shyness and sensitivity.

WHAT's the ratio of introverts to extroverts?

Although estimates vary, many experts believe that roughly

30% of the population is introverted. Some estimates have the figure as low as 25%, while others put it as high as 50%.

But, just to be clear, neither introverts nor extroverts are the same. Many people are ambiverts, meaning they fall somewhere in the middle of the introvert-extrovert spectrum and can thrive in either environment.

Tips for managing introverts

Are you a supervisor or a manager at work? Have you come up with a definition of introversion that corresponds to one of the definitions in this chapter? Creating mental shortcuts and definitions regarding a segment of the population, even one to which you may belong, can easily devolve into pigeonholing and stereotyping, ultimately detrimental to the employee. In truth, each of us is a unique individual.

Here are some things to ask yourself to start dispelling your prejudices about introverts:

- What do I mean when I say introversion?
- How do I react when someone tells me they're an introvert?
- How do I anticipate an introvert behaving?

6

Am I An Introvert?

LET me ask you a question if you're not sure which side of the introvert-extrovert continuum you fall on:

It's Friday, and you've had a very hard week at work. You've worked a long day and are exhausted. What are your plans for the rest of the evening? Do you want to stay at home or go out?

Of course, if you said "go home," you're probably an introvert! However, if being around other people is your idea of a restful weekend, you're most likely an extrovert. You might be an ambivert, someone who falls somewhere in the middle of the spectrum if your response changes depending on your mood. To determine if you're an introvert or an extrovert, look for tendencies and patterns in the way you replenish your energy.

Still, have doubts about whether or not you're an introvert? Here are a few traits that many introverts share:

- Isn't fond of small talk.
- Likes nature.
- Prefers to operate independently rather than as part of a group.
- Gets very enthused and vocal when talking about

something they enjoy but finds it difficult to stay involved in conversations about things they don't care about.
- Has a hard time coming up with quick answers to questions.
- Has sensory overload, which causes discomfort or overwhelms due to too many images, noises, or other stimuli. (If this describes you, you may also be a Highly Sensitive Person on top of being an introvert.)
- After a long period of social interaction, "shuts down" or becomes irritable.
- Doesn't care for open-plan offices.
- Concentrates on work rather than chit-chatting with coworkers.
- Has a small group of close pals.
- Isn't fond of parties.
- Would rather text or e-mail than talk on the phone

Don't worry if only a handful of these characteristics apply to you; introverts come in many forms and sizes. You'll still be able to use this book's ideas and methods to help you succeed in the workplace.

7

The Different Faces Of Introversion

MANY PSYCHOLOGISTS HAVE PREVIOUSLY HIGHLIGHTED the vast range of distinctions between introverts and theories of introversion, which prompted Jennifer O. Grimes, Jonathan Cheek, Julie K. Norem, and Courtney A. Brown to investigate those disparities. They created a survey that had nineteen distinct measures for measuring introversion and extraversion, and they gave it to 225 female students. The hypothesis that there are four forms of introversion—Social, Thinking, Anxious, and Restrained—was born, and the acronym STAR was born. Each of these characteristics can give an introvert a high or low score.

Do you identify with one or more of the types of introverts listed below?

- Smaller gatherings of individuals are preferable to bigger ones for social introverts who cherish their alone time.
- Introverts who think are ruminative daydreamers. They have a penchant for introspection and self-reflection.
- In social circumstances, anxious introverts are self-

conscious. They're also worried at home, contemplating on things they'd prefer to forget.
- It can take a long time for a restrained introvert to get up in the morning. They prefer to take things slowly and consider their options before commenting.

This hypothesis appeals that there is no one-size-fits-all approach to being an introvert—or even to being a human being.

8

Facts About Introverts

IT'S ALL TOO easy to believe that something is wrong with you because you're so different from your outgoing friends. When you're surrounded by social butterflies who mock you about being a "loner" or a "party pooper," it's much easy to feel like an outcast.

But here's the most important takeaway from the book: both innies and outies are fantastic. The world requires both and wise people to understand this. Mother Nature, too, has valid reasons for physiologically wiring innies and outies in different ways.

And here's another fact: you're wonderful as an introvert! You're likely to be a true scholar, a devoted friend, and a creative and independent thinker, as well as a natural-born leader. The following sections give you a closer look at why you're so terrific.

INTROVERTS ARE **great friends**

An extrovert can stroll into a room full of strangers and leave with five new closest friends a few hours later. Making new friends, on the other hand, is difficult for introverts. At first look, it appears that your outspoken pals have the upper hand.

What happens, however, when you do make a new friend? That's where you stick out.

To begin with, you're as devoted as they come. You place high importance on your friendships since you put effort into each one. When disagreements develop, you're more inclined to be forgiving, and you're unlikely to ditch a buddy for someone who's more trendy or fascinating.

A friendship with you lasts a lifetime, and you'll go out of your way to help a friend whenever they need it.

And here's another thing you're good at as a friend: you're a listener, not a talker. So, if one of your pals comes to you with a problem, you'll be willing to listen (as long as they don't go on for too long!). Your introverted friends may be more willing to open up to you than their extroverted counterparts. That's because they know you're considerate and sensitive and that you'll keep their secrets safe.

Would you like another pat on the back? You're not a drama queen or a spotlight-stealer if you're a quiet innie. That guy in the restaurant yelling at his girlfriend? You are not one of them. At your company's holiday party, that woman flaunting her belly-dancing skills? No, that's not you either. Your buddies know you'll never disgrace them in public because you despise making a scene.

INTROVERTS ARE creative

Michelle Pfeiffer, Steven Spielberg, and J. K. Rowling, the author of Harry Potter, all have something in common. Introverts are all three of them. So is Steve Wozniak, Apple co-founder and sole inventor of the original Apple computer.

There are, of course, plenty of creative extroverts. (It's safe to assume that Snoop Dogg is not introverted!) On the other hand, introverts have created some of the world's most beautiful paintings, books, symphonies, scientific theories, and innovations.

Because they can work hard for long periods, introverts thrive at turning creative ideas into reality. Unlike outies, they don't need to stop every several hours and call a friend to recharge their batteries.

Introverts are also thinkers who are self-contained. As a result, they're less likely to go along with the crowd and more likely to come up with novel ideas. This tendency can make things difficult for them in a team-orientated environment, but it also allows them to develop amazing ideas like the light bulb.

Finally, while outies spend much of their time partying, innies spend much of their time learning about the subjects that interest them.

As a result, they're gathering the information they'll need to convert their wild ideas into reality. According to a study that tested college students' knowledge of 20 distinct topics, introverts understood more about each topic than extroverts.

INTROVERTS HAVE a natural ability to lead

In the following chapters, introverted characteristics that can translate into strong leadership qualities are highlighted, such as a willingness to let others shine and a knack for gathering facts and conducting research. Furthermore, many introverts to the top of the leadership chain; these attributes can help you shine as an entrepreneur, mainly if you focus your marketing approach on them. They can also help you manage your way up the corporate ladder utilising a technique known as managing up.

INTROVERTS ARE studious

Are you an introvert with exceptional intelligence or talent? You're not alone if this is the case. Half of the brightest children are introverts, while three-quarters of the "super-gifted" (those with IQs above 160) are innies.

Both introverts and extroverts are intelligent people. Even when their IQs are equivalent, introverts are more likely to thrive in college and acquire graduate degrees.

What is the logic behind this? Introverts are more ready to learn and studying because they enjoy creative interests. They can also focus for longer periods and with greater intensity on complex subjects.

Introverts may also be better at putting off pleasure. So, when they're confronted with a choice like "Should I study for my exam tomorrow or go to a party?" they know what to do. They are more likely than extroverts to make the correct decision.

What has been your previous experience with introverts?

In terms of overall behaviour, how do the introverts encountered differ from one another?

After realising your assumptions and assessing your prejudices, it's much easier to see the introvert in front of you for who they truly are.

9

Determining What Makes You An Introvert

THE CLASSIC ADAGE "KNOW THYSELF" inspired this chapter. It helps to trace your personality back to its beginnings to comprehend your innie nature. Less discuss how you can be true to yourself while also putting on a fake outie face now and again (but only if you want to, because it's your decision). Finally, let's take a deep look into two contentious issues: Is it possible for introverts to become extroverts? Is it a good idea for them to try if that's the case?

IF YOU'RE AN INTROVERT, consider this: Does Mother Nature decide whether you'll be an innie or an outie before you're born? As it turns out, the solution isn't so straightforward. Although there is no singular "introvert gene," there is evidence that the way you display your personality is influenced by where you live and how you were raised.

YOUR GENES

Thank your genes if you have the appearance of a movie star! These genes also influence how tall, short, smart, or athletic you are, as well as whether you have a sweet craving. But how much do they receive credit for your introversion?

The study of twins is one way scientists address this subject. Identical twins share all of their genes, while fraternal twins share only half. Therefore researchers will see a significant difference between the two groups if genes are essential. Scientists can also compare twins who were raised together to twins who were reared separately, which can provide insight into the roles of nature and nurture.

So far, twin studies have shown that genes have a significant impact. It's also evident that no single gene determines whether you're an innie or an outie. Rather, your personality is the outcome of a combination of genes (as well as other factors). Scientists are concentrating their efforts on genes that affect one specific brain chemical: dopamine.

Dopamine is a neurotransmitter that aids in the control of the reward region of the brain. When your slot machine in Las Vegas pours out coins, when you kiss someone, or when you first ski down a slope without landing on your backside, it gives you that "wow" experience. It also says, "Hey, that was a lot of fun!" I want to do that over and over!" As a result, it encourages you to keep pushing that slot machine lever, kissing your sweetheart, or returning to the ski lift.

Many signs suggest that innies and outies have different genes that regulate dopamine levels, activity, and sensitivity. When it comes to meeting new people or trying crazy things like bungee jumping, little differences in particular genes may imply that your extrovert friends receive a higher dopamine thrill than you do. On the other side, they may make you hypersensitive to dopamine, causing you to feel overwhelmed when your environment is bustling with new people and activities.

Furthermore, scientists are investigating the roles of genes that affect other brain chemicals. However, scientists do not know all of the answers when it comes to the effects of genetics on introversion at this time. And there's a lot of disagreement, with today's discoveries frequently contradicting yesterday's. So, while the jury is still out on genes and introversion, those identical and fraternal twins do suggest that heredity plays a significant role.

Your brain's wiring

On the surface, you might be able to tell introverts and extroverts apart if you look around a room. Isn't that guy over there cheerfully flirting with all the ladies? Probably an extrovert. What about the silent guest in the corner with the dog? Most likely, you're an introvert.

But, wait, here's the major question: Can you differentiate innies from outies on the inside by looking at their brain anatomy or wiring? According to scientists, the answer might be yes. Consider the following scenario:

In one study, innies exhibited greater grey and white matter volumes in numerous parts of the brain. They had larger grey matter volume in places that helped them control their behaviour, enabling them to think deeply about themselves and allow them to succeed at social-emotional processing. That's a fancy word for assessing what's happening around you and making inferences about other people's mental states (as in, "What is that guy with the lampshade on his head thinking?").

According to another study, outies have more grey matter on the right side of the brain in a region called the amygdala, which helps them modulate their fear reaction. They also have more grey matter in a part of the brain called the orbitofrontal cortex, which has been linked to a lower risk of depression. This area, according to researchers, may explain why outies are less prone to despair and anxiety.

Another group of researchers discovered that innies exhibit increased activity in the brain regions involved in problem-solving, planning, and recalling events. On the other hand, Outies are more active in areas related to organising and interpreting sensory information.

According to studies, innies and outies' brains react to faces in very different ways. Scientists examined analysed people's brainwaves when they stared at expected or "oddball" (unexpected) faces or flowers in one study. Outies reacted more strongly to the strange faces than to the strange flowers, but innies did not. According to the researchers, this could be proof that introverts can "take or leave" people, which won't surprise you if you're an innie debating whether to attend a party tonight or stay home and read a fantastic book like this one!

And here's something else to think about: Innie and outie brains don't simply react to social cues differently; they also react differently to touch. Researchers evaluated innies and outies' brainwaves while applying fast pressure to their index or pinkie fingers in one investigation. In a brain area that processes information related to touch, innies had stronger responses than outies.

Innies also appear to have heightened taste sensitivity. When introverts and extroverts have lemon juice on their tongues, the introverts salivate more.

What exactly does this imply? It suggests that innies, like highly sensitive people, may be overly sensitive to the input they get from the environment. That may explain why they require more downtime than extroverts who always bounce from one sensory thrill to the next.

The influence of culture

So far, data suggests that biology plays a significant impact in personality development. But wait, there's more to this tale! This is because people's cultures might have an impact on their success as innies or outies.

According to one study, shy or sensitive children in

Canada were evaluated lower than other children. Children in China, on the other hand, gave them a higher rating.

In a separate study, students were assigned to read stories about shy or socially disengaged people. They also asked them to read stories about outgoing and self-assured people. The students were then asked to anticipate how each person will do socially and professionally.

What's the result? Shyness or social disengagement were predicted to harm people's quality of life by students in Western countries significantly more than students in East Asian countries. Furthermore, Westerners who characterised themselves as shy or withdrawn thought that this negatively impacted their lives than shy or withdrawn people in East Asian countries.

As these findings illustrate, thriving can be more difficult in environments where social butterflies are considered normal and introverted or shy persons are considered abnormal.

THE EFFECTS of upbringing

The twin studies mentioned earlier show that genes play a significant role in determining whether or not you are an innie. In comparison, it appears that your family life does not receive nearly as much credit or blame for shaping your personality. However, it turns out that your childhood experiences can still have a significant impact on your life. Why? Because they may be able to anticipate your happiness as an introvert.

If your mother or father is an outgoing person, but you are not, it may be more difficult for you to communicate with them and vice versa. Moving frequently as a child, especially if you're an innie, can increase your chances of being miserable as an adult. That makes sense because innies can find it challenging to adjust to new surroundings and individuals regularly.

Genes and upbringing can also interact, according to

research. 5-HTTLPR is one gene that has gotten a lot of interest. This gene controls the amount of serotonin in the brain. This gene's "short" variation appears to be associated with introversion and a higher risk of depression. However, research suggests that persons with the short variant aren't at an increased risk of depression unless they've been through a traumatic event, such as bullying or abuse. So, supportive families who protect their little ones from traumas (as much as possible) and teach them how to stand up for themselves when bullies attack may help them grow up to be happy adults.

None of this implies that you'll be miserable as an innie if you move around a lot as a kid or that you'll be depressed if you grew up in a troubled family. In reality, even if they moved a lot or grew up in a stressful environment, most innies come out OK. It does, however, demonstrate the importance of family.

And, needless to say, as an innie adult, you'll be happier and more confident if your parents recognise your gifts and understand your requirements. So, even if Mum and Dad don't have much to do with your innie nature, they're critical in how you show it.

10

When Temporarily Playing The Extrovert Can Work To Your Advantage

BEING an innie is ideal in most cases, but it can sometimes put you at a disadvantage. Acting extroverts for a short period may come in handy in certain situations.

Why hide your naughtiness at times? Because in some instances, such as the ones listed below, outies frequently triumph over innies:

- Attracting and retaining customers as an entrepreneur.
- Job interviews.
- Marketing.
- Meetings.
- Networking events.
- Parties.
- Performance reviews.
- Public speaking.

In these brief situations, acting like an extrovert can be beneficial for two reasons. For starters, it can assist you in breaking the ice more quickly, which is advantageous in a brief interaction such as a job interview. Second, it can make you appear more approachable, friendly, and self-assured.

You can put on your outie mask anytime you need it — once a month or once a year — to help you land a dream job, get a promotion, or make a critical networking connection if you add certain pretend-extrovert abilities to your own arsenal. You can tuck it away the rest of the time and be your cheerful innie self.

It's critical to understand that there's no point in strengthening your extrovert muscles if you don't require them. They're entirely needless for many innies. So pay attention to your gut instincts and do what seems right to you.

Mastering the skills of the pretend extrovert

It isn't easy to imagine yourself as the life of the party or as a smooth talker in a job interview. However, if you persistently practice a few pretend-outie abilities, you might surprise yourself! However, mastering these abilities is difficult, so consider whether there is an advantage to you in doing so. If you answered yes, here are the important abilities you should work on.

HONING your body language

People communicate with their words and their movements, such as posture, smiles and frowns, and even the way they move. To play the character of an extrovert, you must imitate outies' body language.

Observing outies in their natural habitat is the best method to master their movements. Keep an eye on the outgoing people the next time you're in a meeting or at a party. Take note of the following details:

- Outies usually stand tall and with their arms apart from their bodies, not crossed over their chests. They lean into the conversation, whether they're speaking or listening. They might bounce a little on their feet because they're so happy or

eager. They also like to listen with their heads raised.
- Innies prefer to preserve a little physical space from other people, but outies may drop down right next to someone on a couch or in a conference room. (Of course, this is dependent on their relationship with the person – try it with your friends, not your employer!)
- Extroverts are more likely to look at someone who is speaking for a longer period, whereas introverts are more likely to look away fast.
- Extroverts tend to make broad gestures and point toward other people, whereas innies tend to gesture at themselves. Outies also make more dynamic and frequent gestures.
- When extroverts grin, they do more than merely raise the corners of their mouths. They crinkle their eyes as well.

Practice extroverted body language at home once you've gotten a feel for it. One entertaining method is to impersonate extroverts in movies or television shows. (Take, for example, Oprah Winfrey, who is a certified outie.)

At initially, mastering the moves of outies will be difficult. "It's like sit-ups — do it every day, and it gets easier," one innie said in an online discussion forum.

BEEFING up your conversational muscles

Introverts possess a variety of skills, but small talk isn't usually one of them. So, if you want to come across as an extrovert in a conversation, you'll have to put in some effort. Practising conversation starters is the greatest way to get started. Here are some of the most effective methods to start a conversation:

Seek counsel from others. If you hear someone talking

about gardening, for example, walk up and say, "I'd like to start a garden of my own, but I'm not sure what grows best around here." Do you have any helpful hints?"

Get people to tell you personal stories. Consider the following scenario:

When speaking with someone who enjoys travelling, ask, "What is the best place you've ever visited?" Worst case scenario?"

If you're talking to a teacher, say something along the lines of, "My sister is a teacher, and she has some wild days." Do things ever get a little out of hand in your class?"

Have you struck up a conversation with a plumber? Inquire about the strangest object he or she has ever pulled from a drain. (Of course, the answer may be something you don't want to hear!)

Starting with a compliment is a great way to get people's attention. Combining your compliment with a question will keep the other person talking for longer. For instance, you could say, "That's lovely jewellery." What store did you get it from?"

Instead of asking questions that individuals can respond to in a few words, ask open-ended questions. Assume you're speaking with a real estate agent. "What part of town has the best house pricing right now?" don't ask. Instead, ask questions like, "How do you feel about the current housing market?"

Don't just stand there and listen once you've started a conversation. Remember, you're playing the part of an outcast! So lean into the conversation, and if the other person cracks a joke, laugh out loud. Also, ask as many follow-up questions as you can stand. (Be patient with yourself as you learn this ability; the more introverted you are, the harder it may be.) Follow-up questions are important because they keep the discussion flowing and show the other person that you're truly interested.

Imagine people's experiences in your head is one of the

best ways to come up with questions to ask them. Imagine yourself as a tourist in Madrid or Barcelona, for example, if the international traveller says she loves Spain. What would you do if you were in that situation? What would you eat if you were hungry? Where would you choose to stay? This might help you come up with various questions to ask her about restaurants, hotels, weather, airports, and other topics. She'll believe you're a natural conversationalist when you're the one doing all the talking.

ROLE-PLAYING WITH A FRIEND

You could be scoffing at the idea of role-playing. It doesn't sound like something an innie would do, does it?

If you decide to try it on your own, the first step is to form a partnership with someone you are very comfortable with. Decide what you want to role-play as well. Role-play meeting a stranger at a party or providing a status update at a meeting, for example.

Try to practice each of the conversational and body language skills as discussed earlier in this chapter in the sections "Honing your body language" and "Beefing up your conversational muscles." It'll be easier if you practice each one separately before attempting to combine them. The more you practice these skills, the easier it will be to use them in real-life circumstances.

STARTING small

If you want to start running, a quarter-mile is a good place to start and work your way up to a marathon. Similarly, it would help if you gave yourself time to hone your impersonation skills before putting them to the test in a high-profile situation.

So start with some simple locations. Make small talk with grocery store clerks, neighbours, or your children's instructors.

Choose larger stages to perform on as you gain more experience playing the outie.

RECOGNISING the pros and cons of being a pretend extrovert

Putting on an outgoing act from time to time can help you advance in your work or social circumstances. Is it, however, beneficial to your mental well-being? It depends, according to researchers.

According to a new study involving college students, acting extroverted made participants — both innies and outies — feel better. The researchers found that acting in an extroverted manner made everyone in their study happier. Another study, on the other hand, came to a different conclusion. It was indicated that while plastering a large extroverted smile on your face may make you joyful; it also has the potential to harm your health.

Researchers encouraged bus drivers to smile at passengers even if they didn't feel like it in this study. They discovered that drivers who forced smiles by the end of the day were emotionally drained and tended to withdraw from other people. For women, the effect was significantly stronger than for men. (However, there is some good news: the same study discovered that bus drivers boosted their mood by reliving happy experiences or thinking about their lives in a more positive light.)

What is the main point to remember? Acting extrovert at times may help you feel better, but it also has the potential to make you feel worse. So give it a shot and keep an eye on the results. Then you can figure out what works best for you.

11

Can You Become A Real Extrovert?

It's one thing to talk about briefly taking on the role of outie when it suits your needs. But here we want to focus on an opposite idea: that an introvert can (and perhaps should) become a genuine extrovert.

This is a complex subject! On the one hand, some advocate for being authentic to oneself. They believe that attempting to convert innies to outies is akin to attempting to convert left-handers to right-handers. Instead, introverts should try to reduce bias towards introverts and increase appreciation for introverts' unique abilities.

On the other side, some believe in "faking it till you make it." It's been suggested that if you're having problems fitting in in a world geared for extroverts, you should change yourself. Their theory is that if you start out pretending to be extroverted and keep practising, you'll eventually realise you're an outie for real — and that you'll like it. They also cite scientific research that suggests that imitating a new habit can gradually become second nature.

Every innie is unique, which means that what works for one person may not work for you at all.

. . .

CAN you truly change your spots?

Scientists are learning that the adult brain is far more "plastic" than previously imagined. This indicates that new experiences can alter people's brain structure as well as their feelings and behaviours.

Is this, however, true of personality? It's an excellent question. When you ask psychologists if it's possible to change your core personality, you'll likely hear several responses. Typically, these responses revolve around one question: Is introversion a fixed trait or a condition that may be changed?

Two of the most prevalent theories are as follows:

- The rubber band hypothesis states that if you stretch a rubber band, you may make it longer, but if you let go, it snaps back. Many psychologists believe that the same is true for innies who want to become outies. They can expand their personalities to a certain extent, but they'll always "snap back" to their inherent innie-ness. Introversion, in other words, is a quality, not a state.
- The situational idea holds that if you're motivated, you can change your personality – at least to some extent. To put it another way, introverts may be able to put their innie tendencies on wait to achieve a goal that is extremely important to them. Introversion is a state, not a feature, according to this idea.

Our experiences demonstrate that whether you want to become more of an outcast or not is entirely up to you. People who say things like "You need to come out of your shell" or "Why can't you be more outgoing like your brother?" should be ignored." If being an innie suit you perfectly, don't change a thing! But if you feel compelled to be more outgoing, that's fine, too.

If you're debating whether or not you want to be more outie, here are a few key measures to consider:

1. Understand yourself.

This book will help you determine whether or not you are genuinely an introvert.

2. Accept yourself completely as you are.

You can then decide whether you want to try edging toward the outie side after that.

MANY PEOPLE REALISE they're innies through when they take these two steps first — understanding yourself and truly accepting yourself — and they're pleased to be that way. On the other hand, others realise they're innies who wish to develop a more outie identity. And, thankfully, both groups get along swimmingly.

If you want to become more of an outcast, pay attention to and respect your feelings. If you find it surprisingly easy to adopt extroverted tendencies, you're an ambivert who can be content as either an innie or an outie. If the pressure of acting outie is draining and exhausting you, it's time to embrace your inner innie and quit pretending to be someone you're not.

WILL you get more innie or outie as you age?

As people grow older, many things alter, including their waistlines and hairlines. Your personality, for example, may change as you get older.

Scientists studied adults aged 21 to 60 years old a few years ago. When they looked at innie and outie behaviour, they discovered that women were less extroverted as they got older, but men did not. A different set of researchers looked at how people changed over 15 years. From their 30s on, both men and women became less extroverted, according to one study.

This finding demonstrates that people are more than the sum of their genes and biology. Clearly, their everyday experiences and the people they interact with have an impact on them.

So don't be surprised if you're more innie at different times in your life. Just go with the flow and know that you'll be alright either way!

12

Introverts In The Workplace

FOR INTROVERTS, the workplace can be full of potential problems. Most of them will have to use a variety of abilities that are outside of their comfort zones. As a result, introverts frequently work alone, at home, or in a profession that allows them to be flexible. However, because not all introverts can create a work environment that is a perfect natural niche, they must understand how to avoid the hazards of a 9-to-5 schedule.

"In space, no one can hear you scream," says a famous sci-fi movie advertisement, but in today's open offices, it's scarier: "In the office, everyone can hear you chat, sneeze, cough, or laugh – or scream."

The lack of privacy in cubicle farms can be a genuine pain for innies. Focusing on rows of data or lines of code can be tough when Jane is shouting with a coworker and Bob is telling everyone about his enlarged prostate. It's also aggravating to know that Jane, Bob, and everyone else in the vicinity can hear every noise you make.

But that's not the only issue you'll have to deal with in an outie-friendly workplace. Here are some more examples:

. . .

The importance of teamwork

Innies are self-starters who like to work alone. Today's office, on the other hand, is based on collaboration. If you work in a standard office, you probably spend your days bouncing from conference calls to team meetings, with little time to think about your tasks alone.

If you're an innie, there are also other risks associated with collaboration. You can find yourself picking up the load for underperforming coworkers because you're inclined to be conscientious (and getting burned out in the process). Alternatively, you could be bullied by aggressive team members who misinterpret your calm demeanour as a lack of confidence.

The demands of multitasking

If you're like most innies, you probably prefer to devote all of your attention to a single project. You might blow a fuse if you try to manage six or seven deadlines. In today's hyper-competitive environment, however, most supervisors want you to multitask effortlessly. You're probably working with near-impossible deadlines, which adds to the stress.

The desire to advertise yourself

As an introvert, you aren't one for boasting about yourself. However, if you don't speak up, you can get lost in a sea of chatty extroverts.

The frequent interruptions

If you work in a regular workplace, you'll be interrupted at least once or twice an hour by someone collecting for a birthday party, asking a question about new software, or requesting your assistance on a project. As a result, your tasks may be thrown off track.

These obstacles can make it tough to advance in the

profession as an innie, and they can also leave you exhausted at the end of the day. Fortunately, there are ways to make your workplace healthier, happier, and more in tune with your innie nature.

Thriving in a Noisy Workplace

The activity of an open office can drain your batteries, leaving you uncomfortable, fatigued, and with a headache. When you feel that way, it's time to escape — at least for a few minutes. Of course, that's easier said than done when you're stuck in a cubicle jungle. But if you're savvy, you can always find a way to take a time-out. The following sections present a few useful suggestions for workplace time-outs.

Making a break for it

When you feel your stress levels mounting, a brief change of environment can do you a world of good. Two or three times a day, get out of the office and take a brisk stroll — or if you're in a building with numerous levels, think of an excuse to run upstairs or downstairs.

When you take your stroll, wear headphones, so you have an excuse to avoid interacting with passers-by. (And if any outies reading this book believe that hiding behind headphones is disrespectful, it's not! It's a survival mechanism for exhausting innies seeking to restore their inner equilibrium.)

Here are some alternative methods to take a micro-vacation from your noisy coworkers:

- Leave the building on your lunch break. If a park is nearby, pack a lunch and soak up a little sunshine as you eat. If not, choose a cosy restaurant or read a book while you eat in your car.
- Offer to fetch bagels for a meeting, pick up documents from another firm, or conduct other

errands. You'll be able to get out of the building for at least a few minutes if you complete these chores. If you're lucky, you might be able to volunteer to run errands on a daily or weekly basis, giving you regular breaks.

CREATING an innie oasis in your cubicle

Here are some of the most effective strategies to put some distance between yourself and your coworkers:

- To help drown out the office noise, invest in noise-cancelling headphones, listen to music, or utilise earplugs. Check with your manager to see whether your organisation has a policy prohibiting the use of headphones or earplugs.
- Use a white noise machine if you want to relax. You may easily get a compact model that will fit inside your cubicle without taking up too much room.
- Make artificial "walls" by stacking books or hanging large photographs on the side of your desk that faces your cubicle door.
- For your cubicle, get a privacy screen. (Ask permission first.) If your firm does not give one, you can purchase one online. It will most likely cost you more than £100, but you may find it to be well worth the money.
- Add some greenery to the mix. Houseplants can help to conceal other people's views of you while also helping to muffle sounds.
- If you can't see the entrance to your cubicle from where you're sitting, put a tiny mirror on your desk so you can see who's approaching.
- Hang a small sign outside your cubicle that says

something like "No interruptions until 2:00, please." when you need uninterrupted thinking time.
- When it comes to the design of your office, could you not make it too cosy for visitors? The message is sent via a candy dish on your desk, which says, "Hello." I'm delighted to see you." A stack of books on your visitor's chair, on the other hand, indicates, "I'd rather be alone." So use your interior decorating skills to communicate clever messages.

SCHEDULING BLOCKS OF "ALONE" time

Do you have some leeway in your schedule? If that's the case, set aside a two- or three-hour block of time to focus solely on your most important assignments. If clients or coworkers want to meet with you during this time, see if they're willing to meet at a later time. Also, make it clear to your boss that you want this time to be as free of distractions as possible.

Also, spend the first 30 minutes of each day dealing with all of the minor things that can detract from your main projects. These hours are often ideal since the office extroverts are too preoccupied with catching up with each other to notice you! As a result, respond to e-mails, make phone calls, and cross small chores off your to-do list. This will free up the brain cells you need to concentrate on the important things.

GETTING physical

If you're an introvert working in a noisy environment, your stress level might quickly rise to the point where you feel ready to crack.

Burning off your stress hormones with some brief exercise

is one of the easiest ways to ease that stress, at least for a short time.

But what about those occasions when you are unable to flee? You can do some stress-relieving activities even if you're locked in your cubicle. Here are some simple activities you may conduct in your cube without drawing attention to yourself:

- Lift one foot an inch or so off the floor while sitting at your workstation. Stretch your leg out in front of you until it is straight. Hold it for a few seconds, then bend your knee while keeping your foot off the floor for a few seconds more. Rep with the other leg, putting your foot back on the floor.
- Put your hands on the chair arms and lift your backside an inch or so off the chair seat if your chair has firm arms. Hold for a few seconds before returning to your chair.
- Alternate raising one hand higher than the other while stretching both arms over your head.

TELECOMMUTING

More companies are accepting the idea of allowing employees to work from home one or two days per week. If yours is one of them, you should consider using this option. It's a fantastic way to unwind after a long day at the office.

If you work from home, make sure to communicate with your coworkers regularly. Send frequent e-mails, keep everyone informed about your progress, and speak out frequently on conference calls. Even if your boss doesn't require daily progress reports, you should send them on days when you work from home. You don't want to be "out of sight, out of mind" when it comes to your business.

Also, for successful telecommuting, follow these guidelines:

- Respond swiftly to e-mails, texts, and instant messaging to let others know you're working.
- Notify your manager and coworkers if you'll be out of the office for lunch or any other reason.
- Define your limits. Quit at the same time you would if you were still at work. (And, in either case, only work overtime when required; else, you'll quickly burn out.)
- Make a distinct work area and inform any family members or roommates that you should not be interrupted while working.

Establishing Yourself at Work

Even if you're an excellent employee who meets every goal and deadline, if you're too modest to speak up, your efforts may be overlooked. It can also be tough to get your thoughts across in meetings, deal with problematic coworkers, or develop connections with the colleagues you want to get to know if you're a quiet introvert.

SHINING a light on your successes

One of the most common complaints from introverts is that they put in the greatest effort yet receive the least praise. What's more, you know what? It's true a lot of the time! Outies aren't afraid to brag about their successes, whereas introverts have a hard time stating, "Look what I did."

Fortunately, you can highlight your accomplishments without going against your introvert's wishes. Here are a few methods:

- Send an e-mail thanking everyone who assisted you at the end of a successful project, with a copy to your supervisor. Outline all of the project's highlights in your e-mail. It will be a lot easier for

you to convey your gratitude to your team than it will be for you to brag about yourself — and your boss will be impressed by both your achievement and your graciousness in thanking your team.
- When you finish a project well, consider whether other people in the firm would benefit from knowing about it. Is it possible that you devised a more efficient method or tried a new software package that proved to be quite beneficial? If this is the case, write to your supervisor and offer to share your information with your coworkers.
- Offer to produce a report for your company's newsletter or blog on your project.
- Also, when it comes to receiving credit for joint projects, be firm. If you're assisting a colleague in creating a PowerPoint presentation for a speech she's giving, for example, make sure the title slide includes both of your names.

FLEXING your quiet power at meetings

Do you have a sinking feeling when you hear the ping of a meeting reminder on your computer? If that's the case, join the horde – the horde of introverts, that is.

Why is it that introverts despise meetings so much? Because they like to listen rather than speak. They have a lot of wonderful ideas, but they don't just come out and say them. They'd rather fine-tune them before sharing them. As a result, they try to say as little as possible in meetings or talk quietly enough that their thoughts are disregarded.

As an introvert, you may also encounter the following annoyances:

- You have a wonderful idea, but it will take you two or three minutes to consider it. Someone else

comes up with the same concept as you're scribbling notes.
- You have a brilliant idea for a contribution ten minutes after the meeting ends, but it's too late, and you spend the next hour blaming yourself for missing a good opportunity.

Meetings will never be enjoyable for introverts (and they aren't always enjoyable for outies), but they will never go away. So the greatest thing you can do is figure out how to use them to your advantage. Follow these guidelines:

- Check to see if you can acquire a schedule ahead of time (or at least get a heads-up about what the meeting will cover). Then, calmly consider the meeting's subjects and jot down your thoughts. This will give you a leg up on the competition. You might come up with new ideas they won't consider because you're probably a deeper thinker than many of the outies in your job.
- When a fresh topic is brought up at a meeting, go first. Introverts don't have instinct, but you'll probably find that it's easier to start a conversation than it is to step into the middle of one.

Memorise a few critical phrases to use in the event of an introvert brain freeze. If you're in a meeting and someone asks you a question, and you're stumped, answer something like this:

- "That's a fascinating question." Can I do some research and send you an e-mail when I'm finished?"
- "I have some ideas, but I'd want to think them over a little more." Is it possible for us to meet together later and chat about it?"

If you can't get a word in edgewise in an outie-dominated meeting, send an e-mail with your points. Say something like, "Carl's new logo concept is excellent, and I think we can make it pop even more if we utilise these new packaging colours." Keep your e-mails focused and confident.

TIPS FOR AVOIDING e-mail mistakes

If you're a strong writer, like many introverts, e-mails may be preferable over face-to-face encounters. If that's the case, make sure you're getting the most out of this communication tool. Here are some hazards to stay away from:

Being overly wordy: If you send extensive e-mails, consumers are more likely to skim through them and overlook important information. So keep your e-mails short, or if you must send a long message, make crucial topics stand out by highlighting them in yellow.

Being excessively terse: A brief response can easily be misinterpreted as harsh or angry. So, if a coworker informs you he's finished a project, instead of writing back, "Okay," add, "Okay — and thanks again for your hard work on this."

Being ambiguous: To avoid any misunderstanding, look at your e-mail from the recipient's perspective and make sure what you're asking, recommending, or agreeing to is crystal clear.

Using capital letters to stress a point: This is a massive no-no since it makes you appear abrasive and unpleasant. Italicising words is fine as long as you don't go overboard.

Avoid using happy faces and LOLs in your e-mails unless your workplace is extremely laid-back.

If you're angry with a coworker, you might be inclined to send a caustic e-mail straight away. But resist the temptation! Instead, turn off your computer and write your response on a piece of paper or in your word document. Then, after a few hours or maybe a day has passed, re-read your words once you've calmed down. You'll likely decide to tone down your rant.

Warning: If you do decide to respond right immediately, make sure to remove the recipient's e-mail address from your message while you're writing it. Otherwise, you risk sending your message before carefully considering what you want to say.

STANDING up to workplace troublemakers

If you're lucky, the majority of your coworkers will be wonderful people to work with. However, you may come across some rotten eggs from time to time. Here are three of the most troublesome employees and how to deal with them.

Bullies

Bullies aren't just found on playgrounds. They're especially common in offices, where their obnoxious demeanour can ruin your day and prevent you from finishing your work.

If you can, avoid these bullies; if you can't, handle them with care. Bullies in the workplace can wield a lot of authority. If you irritate them, they may try to destroy your plans.

If a bully starts ranting at you, don't fight back, but don't give up either. Instead, utilise the defusing process, which entails the following steps:

1. Allow the individual to vent.

"It sounds like you're pretty irritated that we changed this software code," for example, and then let the other answer. Listen quietly for many minutes, no matter how angry he is until he begins to calm down.

2. Restate what he said using the person's name.

"Mike, if I'm getting this right, you're furious because I altered this code without consulting you," for example.

3. Suggest a course of action.

"I have a suggestion about how we can address this," you say, and then list your ideas.

A bully will usually start to back down if you apply this strategy often. Go to your management if he continues to push you about. If it doesn't work — or if the bully is your boss — go to your HR department about the situation.

STEAMROLLERS

Steamrollers are those obnoxious coworkers that talk over or disregard other people in meetings. Introverts typically sit and fume as extroverts fight their way back into the conversation.

If a steamroller keeps interrupting meetings, your boss should step in. However, if this does not occur, you must take matters into your own hands. Take out a piece of paper, write down what you want to say, and hand it over to the steamroller when he interrupts you or refuses to allow you to have the floor. This action will usually cause him to come to a halt and pay attention to you. And if you repeat this process often enough, he'll ultimately learn to be quiet while you speak.

TIME-SUCKERS

The time-sucker is a problematic coworker you're bound to meet at some point. This person keeps interrupting your job with silly queries, minor grievances, or pleas for assistance. You may have difficulty saying no to time-suckers as an introvert since you are sensitive. However, it's equally critical to keep these folks from exploiting you.

So, if you see a coworker is wasting an inordinate amount of your time, use the following strategies:

Make a line. "I'd love to talk about this," you may respond, "but the only time I have is tomorrow between 8:00 and 8:15."

Return the favour by making your demands. "I'd be happy to assist you with your endeavour, Judy," say something along these lines. But, because I'm so busy, I'll need you to help me with this financial report. Is it all right with you?" After a few times, your time-sucker will most likely quit bothering you. (Practicing your approach on a friend or partner beforehand will help you be more forceful if you're an introvert.)

MAKING allies in the workplace

It's more enjoyable to work with people you like, and having allies at work makes it simpler to get things done. When you get along with your coworkers, they are more inclined to assist you out, listen to your ideas, and solve difficulties.

It may be difficult for you as an introvert to make friends with your coworkers. However, if you have a plan, it isn't all that difficult. The first stage is to pick a few people you'd like to be friends with and allies with, then direct their attention to them in the following ways:

However, you may be considering a change of career. If that's the case, you're not alone! Most people nowadays change careers at least a couple of times before reaching retirement age.

But here's a question: If you're introvert thinking about changing careers, are there any better options than others? In this section, You get some answers and clarify how to choose the perfect vocation for you.

13

Jobs That Appeal To Introverts And Extroverts

DEFINING any vocation as off-limits for introverts is a mistake. In actuality, some introverts thrive when they push the introvert envelope, while others thrive when they stay true to their "inner introvert." Still, some jobs are better suited to introverts than others.

As you go through the following lists, keep in mind that no job is entirely introvert - or outie-focused. However, in general, some jobs allow you to follow your introvert desires the majority of the time, while others oblige you to play the extrovert persona.

JOBS FOR INTROVERTS

Here are a few examples of jobs where introverts can apply their skills. These jobs typically need you to think critically, work independently, or meet with people one-on-one.

- Accountant or bookkeeper
- ATC (Air Traffic Control)
- Airline pilot
- Auditor
- Carpenter

- Data entry technician
- Dog groomer
- Engineer
- Rancher or farmer
- Farmer or rancher
- Graphic designer
- Janitor
- Landscaper
- Librarian
- Mail deliverer
- Market researcher
- Medical biller or coder
- Technician in a medical laboratory
- Paralegal
- Photographer
- Worker in a plant nursery
- Plumber
- Scientist
- Software developer
- Tax or trust attorney
- Truck driver
- Writer, editor, or translator

Because they are sensitive and have excellent listening abilities, Introverts can become excellent psychologists and psychiatrists. Many introverts flourish in other one-on-one medical settings, such as physical or speech therapy, for the same reason. Many introverts also enjoy working in home health care or hospice, where they can build close ties with a small number of patients at a time.

Jobs more suited for outies

Some jobs may be difficult for introverts to complete. Working in teams, meeting a lot of new people, making small conversations, and even getting confrontational are all common occurrences in these positions. Here are a few occupations that will require you to apply some of the pretend-outie talents:

- Customer service representative
- Defence lawyer
- Grocery clerk
- Hairstylist
- Hospital nurse
- Police officer or firefighter
- Politician
- Estate Agent
- Salesperson
- Sports coach or trainer
- Telemarketer
- Wedding planner

YOU SHOULD CONSIDER your introverted personality while choosing a job sector, but you should also choose one that aligns with your interests and talents. So, how can you figure out which option is best for you? If you're not sure, examine the following questions:

What is your level of introversion? If you're only somewhat introverted, you might be a good fit for an outie job. If you're a true introvert, however, it'll be a lot more difficult.

Try to gain a solid sense of where you genuinely fit on the introvert-outie scale as you go through this book. Also, figure out which introvert characteristics apply to you. Do you, for example, despise speaking in front of groups or enjoy giving speeches? Do you despise commotion, or are you able to tune it out? Your responses can help you figure out which job path is best for you.

How intensely does one profession entice you? If you have a great talent or a strong passion, it will almost certainly lead you to the career that is suitable for you, even if it doesn't fit your personality. Because acting is in their DNA, some introverted actors grit their teeth and put up with all the promotional shots and Hollywood parties. Some extroverts shut themselves away for hours penning volumes about the War of 1812 because history fascinates them.

ARE you willing to take a chance and fail?

If you wish to pursue an outie profession, proceed in the same manner. Recognise that it's a risk, and congratulate yourself on trying it, even if it doesn't pan out.

Do you need a wake-up call? People frequently choose a career field because it appears to be a wonderful match for their skills and characteristics, only to learn that the job isn't at all what they imagined. Shadowing someone in the field you're interested in is one approach to avoid this issue. This can assist you in determining whether or not that career is a good fit for your personality.

Are you self-assured enough to defend yourself? You may need to adjust your outie employment to match your demands to prosper. As a result, you must be willing to talk honestly about your requirements – not only with your coworkers but also with your supervisor. Consider whether you have the fortitude to go through with it. If that's not the case, an introvert-friendly job would be a better fit.

As you consider your employment alternatives, consider which ones will provide you with the most freedom. Some occupations require you to work in an office, while others allow you to work from home for part or all of the time. Many professions can allow you to work on your own as an entrepreneur.

14

Introvert With Leadership Skills

AN UNUSUAL STEREOTYPE holds that the most effective executives are strong, fast-talking extroverts in the business world. Try saying it to Bill Gates, Warren Buffett, or Charles Schwab, all of whom are proven introverts.

On the other hand, introverts are frequently the finest leaders, especially when they play to their strengths.

YOUR RESEARCH and decision-making skills

One of your biggest talents as an innie is your ability to analyse topics thoroughly. You're not readily swayed by the loudest voice in the room, unlike outies who occasionally act without considering all the facts. Instead, you're more likely to gather all of the information before making a judgment.

You're also inclined to be careful while making decisions, unlike extroverts who typically act on gut alone. Even if you have a gut feeling that you should do something, you'll ask yourself, "Why do I have that feeling?"

Furthermore, you aren't a "my way or the highway" type of person. You make decisions that benefit your team or company, not what pleases your ego or puts you in the spotlight.

. . .

Your knack for encouraging independence

Innies are independent thinkers who urge those around them to do the same. A recent study indicated that introverts are frequently stronger leaders than extroverts when it comes to allowing their subordinates to think outside the box.

The researchers looked at the personalities of shop managers of a nationwide pizza delivery chain in the first section of this study. They also decided whether each store's employees were go-getters who spoke up, recommended improvements, and shared their thoughts with supervisors or if they were only doing their jobs. (The first group was designated "proactive," while the second was branded "passive.") Finally, they looked at the profitability of each store.

What did they discover? Stores with passive staff had more extroverted managers, while stores with aggressive employees had more introverted managers.

The researchers next asked college students to fold shirts to put innie and outie leaders to the test differently. There was one leader and four followers in each group. What the kids didn't realise was that one of each group's followers was an actress. In some groupings, the actors just folded their shirts with the rest of the group. Others devised ingenious ways to speed up the folding process.

With an outgoing leader, the shirt-folders in the passive groups did a little better. However, in groups, when someone stated, "I have a better idea; can we try it my way?" things were dramatically different. "In this scenario, extroverted leaders fought fresh ideas while introverts listened. As a result, when introverted individuals led the proactive groups, they folded more shirts than when an outie leader led them.

What is the message being conveyed here? Both extroverted and introverted leaders are capable of accomplishing their goals. However, if you want to maintain your company ahead of the curve, pairing a team of brilliant, motivated employees with an introverted leader who will let them shine might be your best choice.

15

Anticipating The Difficulties Of Leading As An Introvert

ONE OF YOUR strong points is that you're willing to face the facts (even if they're unpleasant) head-on. So now it's time to look into some of the potential stumbling blocks for you as an innie leader.

Here are the challenges that most introverts-in-charge face.

People may misinterpret your introversion as arrogance or aloofness. People may not tell when you're interested and caring because you're not a great talker and don't always display your feelings on your face.

Others may misinterpret your introversion as a lack of self-assurance. Your quiet personality and habit of thinking before speaking may make you appear cautious in an outie office that encourages people to speak out and make rapid judgments, which might translate into less respect and fewer promotions.

It might be difficult to find the quiet moments you need to recharge your batteries when your daily calendar involves meetings, interviews, speeches, fundraisers, and other people-packed activities. You may have difficulties focusing, feeling agitated, or even developing medical symptoms if you don't get enough "alone" time. (Common complaints include headaches and indigestion.)

Multitasking can be exhausting. Introverts prefer to focus on one item at a time, but this isn't an option as a leader. You'll not only be juggling a lot of chores; you'll also be dealing with various crises at times. This might cause a lot of anxiety, especially if you're naturally sensitive.

You might overlook some crucial information. Introverts can tune out speakers when they think a topic is unnecessary because they don't like a small conversation. When this happens, individuals risk missing critical information or offending the people with whom they're conversing.

In short, leading as an introvert isn't always easy. However, when you chat with extroverts, you'll find out that they have their own set of problems. (For example, even when they aren't, they can be perceived as aggressive, overbearing, or shallow.)

In the end, being an innie or an outie isn't an ineffective factor in leadership. Instead, learning the leadership abilities that allow your inner strengths to show is the key.

Setting the Stage for Success

People often consider those at the top of the organisational structure to be natural leaders. But, whether they're introverts or extroverts, many of the world's most successful CEOs and managers had to work hard to build the talents that brought them where they are. Building the correct set of leadership skills — skills that helped hundreds of introverted and extroverted leaders acquire — will help you overcome any obstacles that are preventing you from advancing in your profession. These same abilities can help you become a great communicator, a terrific motivator, and an inspiration to your team. The following are the most crucial steps to being a successful leader.

. . .

BUILDING your transformational skills

Many business leaders follow a simple formula for attaining results: they reward staff for good performance and punish them for poor performance. That's transactional leadership, and it has a place in the world. (After all, it's a safe bet that if you didn't pay your employees, they wouldn't show up and work hard every day!)

On the other hand, successful leaders prepare for the long term, which necessitates a different strategy: convincing others to believe in your aims and values. This is transformational leadership, and it's the kind that can set you apart from the competition. Transformational leadership goes beyond maintaining the status quo and helps you to build high-performing teams full of new ideas and energy.

According to research, extroverts are better at transformative leadership than introverts because extroverts are more charismatic and open to sharing their ideas. This leadership style, however, may be mastered by anyone, innie or outie.

The major steps are outlined in this section:

- Create an inspiring vision and let your people know they're crucial to achieving it.
- Get your team's input first to get them interested in your vision. Outline your goal and invite each team member to think of five ways they may contribute to making it a reality. Simultaneously, come up with your ideas.
- Then, set up a brainstorming session so everyone may contribute their thoughts. Agree on concrete approaches to accomplishing your objective at the end of the meeting.

For example, if you're working with a hotel's housekeeping staff, your vision could be, "In addition to cleaning, we brighten each guest's day a little." And the specifics you agree on could include:

- Fluffing guests' pillows.
- Leaving extra washcloths.
- Using guests' names when speaking with them.
- Keeping hallway conversations quiet while working.
- Encourage your people to come up with their ideas and solutions.
- Say something like, "How can we improve this design?" regularly." or you come up with a better way to do it?" Reward people for their ingenuity and inventiveness, and allow them to take certain chances.

Have clear expectations

Keep your employees striving for more significant goals, but make sure they're attainable. And make those objectives crystal clear! Unstated expectations, miscommunicated expectations, and unrealistic expectations are the leading reasons for unhappiness in businesses. So let your colleagues know exactly what you want and don't be too severe on them because of your innie perfectionist streak.

Also, even if you're an overachiever yourself, realise that even your best performers won't be as enthusiastic about your goals as you are, so don't expect them to be workaholics. (Keep in mind that some employees work smarter rather than harder!)

Walk the walk

Be a role model if you want to build a high-performing team. Work as hard as (or even harder than) your teammates, speak up for them, and give them credit for your accomplishments.

. . .

BE A MENTOR

Develop your team members' skills and look for opportunities to help them advance professionally. Also, assist them in learning from their mistakes and navigating through difficult situations.

16

Reinforcing Effectively

ALTHOUGH TRANSFORMATIVE LEADERSHIP can propel your team to new heights, plain old-fashioned incentives should also be part of your toolkit. And knowing a little about reinforcement will help you reward your employees more effectively.

PRACTISING positive and negative reinforcement

As a leader, you have two options for reinforcement: positive and negative.

When people perform well, positive reinforcement implies praising them in some way. You may receive increases, incentives, or promotions as a result of your efforts. You can also provide incentives such as these:

Praising people for their contributions both publicly and privately: This is something that both innie and outie leaders tend to ignore. On the other hand, Praise should be at the top of your priority list because recognition is often just as valuable to an employee as money. (And it's free!) Compliment your high performers in departmental e-mails or feature them in your corporate newsletter, in addition to verbal recognition.

Just make sure your compliments are specific and relevant to their work.

OFFERING EXTRA PERKS AND PRIVILEGES: For example, if one of your employees works her tail off to complete a project on schedule, consider rewarding her with an afternoon off to attend her child's sports day.

OFFERING PLUM ASSIGNMENTS: Your finest employees work hard to make you happy, so reward them by assigning them projects they enjoy. Just make sure you lay out your criteria for receiving those assignments — and make sure to recognise not only your top performers but also those who work hard and support your team.

THE FLIP SIDE of the reinforcement coin is negative reinforcement. This style is often misunderstood as punishment, yet it is not. Negative reinforcement is defined as "increasing the behaviour you want to see by taking away something unpleasant when the person exhibits the desired behaviour."

Consider Brandon, a high-school student who is enrolled in algebra. For the first several months, he slacks off, and his teacher summons him for a meeting. "Right now, you're probably going to get a D in this class," she says. Brandon thinks to himself, "Yikes! I know you don't want that since you're expecting to go into a decent college in a few years." I don't want to earn a D," he says, so he works incredibly hard for the next several months and gets a B from his teacher. Because he avoided the D, this is negative reinforcement.

Negative reinforcement, however, is not limited to slackers. One of the finest ways to provide negative reinforcement as a middle manager is to act as a buffer between your team and unpleasant upper-level bosses. Taking away something unpleasant, such as reprimands from above, instils stronger devotion in your people, and managers who do this are unsung heroes.

Reinforcing (or punishing) like a pro

Keep this tip in mind when using reinforcement: "Think like Las Vegas." Imagine yourself in front of a slot machine in a casino to get a sense of what we are talking about. What keeps you yanking on the lever? Uncertainty. You have no idea how many pulls it will take to achieve a reward. And, unless you have a strong enough resolve, that uncertainty will have you testing your luck over and over again.

The same is true when it comes to reinforcing your personnel. You can keep your employees guessing about when they'll get their next incentive if you reinforce in an unpredictable way (a practice psychologists call intermittent reinforcement). As a result, they'll put forth the extra effort to earn it.

On the other hand, when you punish, you want to be consistent. If you dock an employee's pay for being late, for example, do it every time.

Be careful to reward far more frequently than you penalise. Otherwise, your workforce will be disillusioned, and your top performers will be forced to depart.

Mastering the art of structured brainstorming

It's a safe bet that you'll spend a lot of your time brainstorming in today's corporate world. As a leader, you'll most likely be in charge of many of these sessions. If that's the case, do things a little differently than most leaders.

The traditional brainstorming method is to gather your team in a room, present the problem(s) you're trying to solve, and invite them to share any ideas or suggestions that come to mind (no matter how silly or crazy they think it is). You write down whatever they say without critiquing it as they do so. Your team's mission is to come up with new and innovative concepts.

Does this method work? Well, yes and no. And as an introvert, you can probably guess why.

In a brainstorming session, you'll usually hear a lot from your extroverts but not from your introverts. Brainstorming sessions can exhaust innies to the point of shutting them down. As a result, you're missing out on a lot of the information you need. Instead, use a technique known as structured brainstorming. This is a method for bringing out the best in both your innies and outies. Here's how to go about it:

1. Give each group member a piece of paper and encourage them to jot down their thoughts on why a problem arises and how they can address it.

As with traditional brainstorming, advise your group to jot down even the most ridiculous ideas. Tell them that you'll call on them to contribute at least one of their ideas in a few minutes.

2. After everyone has finished writing, walk around the room and ask everyone to share their thoughts.

If they say that other people have already voiced their thoughts, inquire about which ones they liked best.

3. Open the floor for debate once everyone has had an opportunity to offer at least one proposal. This will allow participants to expand on their suggestions or contribute to their understanding of other people's ideas.

. . .

THIS STRATEGY IS effective because it gives both innies and outies a voice. Starting with a pen and paper allows introverts to ponder their ideas in peace. (And by stating that each individual must submit at least one idea, you are encouraging your introverts to speak up.) After that, everyone has a chance to speak. Finally, you give the extroverts a chance to speak up and make more opinions. As a result, you'll hear from everyone on your team, not just the loudmouths.

17

Boosting Your Emotional Intelligence

WHY DO some leaders with average competence and intelligence achieve spectacularly, while others with higher IQs and more excellent talent fail miserably? Emotional intelligence is a quality that many great leaders excel at (or EI). Here's a rundown of what EI is and how to improve it.

UNDERSTANDING EI and why it matters in the workplace

Emotional intelligence (EI) is a fancy word for something that isn't difficult. It's the ability to recognise, comprehend, and control your own and other people's emotions.

Emotional intelligence is described in various ways, but the Mayer-Salovey-Caruso Emotional Intelligence Test is the most accurate (or MSCEIT). It focuses on the following four characteristics of EI:

- Increasing your awareness of your own and others' emotions.
- Emotions in decision-making: How to Use Them Effectively.
- Becoming aware of emotional chain reactions.

- Being able to manage your own and other people's emotions successfully.

The higher your emotional intelligence, the better you get at all four of these skills. As a result, you'll enjoy the following advantages:

- You'll be able to deal with conflicts far more effectively.
- People you manage will be more motivated to help you reach your objectives.
- You'll be able to express yourself more clearly.
- You'll have more negotiating power.
- You'll be better at leading others through difficult situations.
- You'll be better at spotting and supporting your top performers.
- You'll improve your ability to recognise the wants of your clients or consumers.
- Your turnover rate will decrease.

When you improve your own EI, you may also improve your ability to spot job candidates with a high EI. This is critical since these individuals can improve your team's performance. According to one study, sales assistants with high EI produce twice as much money as their lower-EI counterparts, and programmers with extremely high EI scores develop software three times faster than their lower-EI counterparts.

18

Raising Your Own Emotional Intelligence

IF YOU'RE like most individuals, you're an expert in some areas of EI but not so much in others. However, with a little effort, you can improve your EI. Here are some ideas for how to go about it:

- Make contact with your feelings. Take some time to consider how you react to your coworkers or happenings at work, and see if any patterns emerge. How do you deal with pressure? To squabble? To irritate others? Examine your strengths and shortcomings to see if you can spot them.
- Recognise the sources of your stress. Consider the last three or four times you've lost control. Can you pinpoint why you "fell apart" – and come up with a better response?
- Understand what motivates you. Make a list of your objectives and values. You'll be more in touch with your own emotions after realising what matters most to you and why.
- Learn how to lean into debates. When someone starts whining or ranting, your natural reaction

becomes defensive, especially if you're an introvert. High-EI leaders, on the other hand, encourage the furious person to keep talking by saying things such as, "Can you tell me more about that?" or "You appear to be disturbed; could you tell them what happened that bothered you the most?" They then ask other questions while calmly listening to the replies. You'll be astonished at how quickly you can transform a furious tirade into a peaceful chat if you try it.

- Allow yourself to be influenced by other people's opinions. People tend to tune out opposing viewpoints, but this is a low-EI tactic that can keep your mind closed to fresh ideas. Find a news programme or radio broadcast that you actively despise and watch (or listen) for at least an hour to help you become more receptive to listen to diverse points of view. As you do so, don't only think to yourself, "That individual is so foolish!" Instead, ask yourself, "What common ground can I find with this person?" or "I completely disagree."

- Put yourself in the shoes of others. If Joe, your office assistant, yells at you, don't lash out right away. Instead, consider what he's going through. Have you inadvertently stepped on his toes, belittled him, or overworked him? Or is he dealing with personal issues like a divorce or illness? See if you can get to the bottom of Joe's behaviour by looking past your upset feelings.

- Pay attention to people's body language. Keep an eye on people's faces, postures, and gestures when you're speaking with them, especially if they're upset. People's body language frequently sends messages that their words do not.

- Look for safe ways to let off anger. When you're angry or hurt, resist the impulse to say whatever comes to mind or to write that e-mail you'll come to regret. Instead, say, "I'd like to think about this and come back to you later." Find a quiet spot and write down all of your emotions on paper, then destroy it. You'll feel less enraged and be able to talk about the problem more sensibly if you do this.

Mastering the art of focused conversation

You're probably better at one-on-one conversations than you are at speaking in front of a group as an innie. So, in addition to large meetings, search for opportunities to meet with each member of your team individually. When you do, you can utilise a method known as a focused discussion to make the most of your time together. Here's a look at how to use this strategy.

DEFINING **focused conversation**

A concentrated conversation is a technique for delving deeply into subjects from a variety of perspectives. Consider it as a method of probing a topic's depths from the surface. It's a technique that works effectively in both one-on-one conversations and group discussions.

A focused conversation provides you with a clear plan to follow and allows you to collect the most information in the least amount of time. Furthermore, it goes beyond simply gathering information and lets you evaluate the data to make informed judgments.

FOLLOWING **the steps of a focused conversation**

The Institute of Cultural Affairs devised a four-step

strategy for a focused discourse to enable various groups to work together productively.

FACT-GATHERING: This is the stage in which you collect data. For example, if Dave is working on a marketing campaign, you can inquire about how long it will take him and what materials he plans to use.

Reflecting: You can get a sense of Dave's feelings about his endeavour by looking at this section. For instance, you may ask, "What do you think the main problem in this campaign is?" or "Do you think this campaign will be more successful than the previous one?"

Interpreting: This is a wonderful area to ask *why* questions when interpreting. "Why do you believe the last campaign didn't do well?" you can ask Dave. or "How do you think our focus group responds to this new slogan?"

You and Dave make decisions about how to proceed with the project at this stage. You can answer questions such as, "What additional components should we add to our campaigns in the future?" here. or "How can we use social media to reach out to even more people?"

Recap: Go over the main topics at the end of the chat and make sure you both agree on the next steps.

19

Introverts And Public Speaking

Do you get nervous just thinking about standing out in front of a crowd? If that's the case, welcome to the club! When millions of usually confident people consider walking in front of an audience, their knees turn to jelly.

On the other hand, introverts typically make the best public presenters and seminar leaders, which may surprise you. Because innies are usually very informed and passionate about their issues and know how to put together good presentations, this is the case. Furthermore, even the most introverted individuals can overcome their aversion to public speaking. Many innies learn to appreciate public speaking with practice! (I, for one, am one of them.)

To get you started, let's see some pointers on preparing yourself before giving a speech.

Calming Your Innie Nerves: Preparation Is the Key

The majority of people believe that adequate preparation is the most important factor in becoming a confident and successful speaker. Whether you're giving a half-hour keynote or a full-day course, this is true.

. . .

THE PARTS that follow look at the best strategies to set the groundwork for a successful presentation.

VISUALISING success

When you hear the word "preparation," you usually think of writing down and preparing your speech. But boosting your self-esteem and overcoming negative ideas are equally important. Visualisation is one of the most effective methods for accomplishing this. This remarkable tool is used by virtually all of the world's finest athletes, and it's an important element of the work done with professional athletes.

What is the power of visualisation? Researchers divided collegiate basketball players into three groups in one experiment. For a month, they asked one group to shoot free throws for one hour each day. The second group was asked to imagine shooting and making free throws without ever touching a basketball. The third group did not participate in any of the activities.

As you might expect, the third group did not improve their free-throw shooting. The group that shot free throws physically, on the other hand, improved their shooting by 24%. But here's the kicker: the group that just imagined themselves hitting free throws improved by 23%! In other words, visualisation was nearly as effective as shooting baskets.

Fortunately, what works for athletes also works for the majority of the population.

HERE ARE some of the most effective visualisation techniques to attempt in the days leading up to your presentation:

- Visualise your desired outcome. Consider yourself after your lecture or seminar, enjoying the acclaim of your audience. Consider how relieved you are that it is over!

- Visualise yourself completing critical milestones on your way to achieving your objective. Imagine giving a beautiful opening speech, earning a chuckle when you tell a hilarious anecdote, and having people approach you afterwards to ask questions and applaud your performance.
- Anchoring is something you should practice. You recognise any bad pictures in your head, such as tripping over your words or forgetting your speech, using this visualisation technique. Then, you choose a specific sight, sound, or sensation to replace it for each negative image. Rosalyn Fairbank, for example, convinced herself that the hostile crowd at the French Open was cheering for her instead of her opponent. (And it paid off: she won the French Open Doubles twice.) Similarly, if you catch yourself imagining failure, replace it with the sound of applause from your audience.
- Visualise yourself in the room where you'll be speaking throughout your visualisation exercises. If you have access to one, practise your speech in the actual room. Practice your speech in the conference room where you'll be speaking, for example, if you're giving a presentation to a group of managers at your firm. On the day of your speech, the look of the room will prompt your mind to recall the stuff you've prepared.
- When it comes to pictures, many people have distinct mental methods. Some people like to imagine huge things, such as a hundred people congratulating them after a speech. This image provides them with an extra jolt of confidence, they say. (And who knows, maybe it will!) On the other hand, others conjure up more modest dreams of achievement, believing that these are

more feasible. Choose the method that works best for you.

It's a good idea to keep your visualisation sessions on a daily routine. If you're nervous the day before your presentation, repeat your visualisation exercises two or three times that day and add coping statements like, "I know the content better and more thoroughly than everyone else in the room." It won't be a problem for me." On the day of your talk, the more opportunities you have to imagine achievement, the better off you'll be.

IDENTIFYING your pivotal points

When people first begin giving speeches, they often believe that they must be flawless from beginning to end. As a result, they obsess over every word, movement, and PowerPoint slide. However, if you can nail down a few important components of your speech, or critical themes, the rest will come into place. Look for your own critical points while you practice your speech. Do you find that if you start strolling about the room as you deliver your speech, it works better? Or do you notice that after you break the ice with a terrific anecdote, your words flow easily? If that's the case, develop a list of these crucial areas and concentrate on them. You'll feel more sure about your speech once you've pinpointed them.

Mastering your material

You'll sound calmer and collected on the big day if you spend more time polishing your presentation. Rehearsing your speech also aids you in identifying and correcting any flaws. As a result, remember the age-old adage: practice, practice, practice! Here's how to perfect your presentation.

ORGANISE YOUR IDEAS

Your mind will be racing with ideas for your speech at first. To tame those ideas and get them to fall into a logical order, start working on your speech as soon as you learn that you'll be giving it.

To acquire a hold on your material, figure out what kind of presentation you'll be giving. A keynote speech usually lasts about 30 minutes. In contrast, a workshop or seminar can run anywhere from half a day to several days. Know how much time you have and what topics you'll be covering.

Also, be aware of the context of your presentation. If you're making a speech at a conference, find out what the conference's overarching topic is so you can modify your presentation and make references to it. Ensure you know what the organisers want you to cover if you're hosting a workshop or seminar.

Next, decide what kind of presentation you'll give. It will most likely fall into one of the following three categories:

- **Informative:** The goal of this style of discussion is to share your knowledge. A speech discussing your company's current financial situation is a fantastic example. Your main goal here is to make your speech as clear and engaging as possible.
- **Technical:** This is a "how-to" presentation in which you demonstrate a skill to your audience. In this scenario, being clear, truthful, and interesting is your first goal.
- **Persuasive:** In this sort of presentation, you're pitching an idea, a proposed change, or a product or service to your audience. The most important thing for you to do now is to get people to buy in.

It's also a good idea to come up with a working title at this time. It may not be the final product, but it will point you on the correct path. Start with "Five Ways to Increase Your Customer Base," for example.

Now that you have this information, you may begin gathering material for your presentation. If you prefer high-tech tools, gather and keep your information on whatever device suits you best.

Keep a supply of sticky notes on you at all times so you may jot down ideas as they occur to you. At this point, don't edit or critique your ideas; simply get them down on paper. Add them to your file at the end of the day. If you're stuck for ideas, go online and search for articles on LinkedIn or other websites.

While working on your speech, it's also a good idea to keep a recording device in your car or a notepad by your bed. Some of your best ideas may come to you while you're driving or late at night.

Create your dump sheet

Create a dump sheet when you think you have enough material to start roughing out your speech. (Journalists coined the term "dump sheet" to describe the process of "throwing out" thoughts on paper many years ago.)

The following are the benefits of creating a dump sheet:

- It enables you to determine what you know and don't know about your subject.
- It assists you in identifying your biases.
- It causes your brain to move to the frontal lobe, allowing you to think logically. This will assist you in overcoming your fear and identifying the practical steps you must take to make your presentation a success.
- It assists you in identifying potential queries from your audience.

If you just have a week to prepare your speech, start with your dump sheet and then gather the materials, you'll need to fill in the gaps.

Use your dump sheet to assist you in answering questions such as the following:

- What knowledge do I have on the subject?
- What do I know about this subject that you don't?
- To fill up the gaps, what more study do I need to conduct?
- What is it about the material that I find most appealing?
- What should I concentrate on?
- What are the main points I want to discuss?

Find a quiet time and hide somewhere with a pen and paper or your laptop to make your dump sheet. Then jot down any thought that occurs to mind about your subject. At this point, don't censor your thoughts. Use a stream-of-consciousness approach instead.

Use index cards

After you've completed your dump sheet, record each of your ideas on an index card, or make "virtual" cards using storyboarding software or PowerPoint presentations. Leave some additional space at the top of each card so you may add keywords later. (You can alternatively use sticky notes on a felt board.)

Here's what to do next if you're using real or virtual index cards:

1. Go through your cards and write a few keywords at the top of each one to explain the information on the card.

Consider the top three to five critical points you discovered from your dump sheet when you do this.

2. Sort your cards, so that cards with related keywords are near one other.

Arrange your cards in a logical arrangement until they start to fall into place. (If you have some blank spots at first, don't worry.)

3. To DEFINE YOUR "OPENERS" and "closers," add cards.

Consider what you can say to make your audience laugh while you're in one of these locations. Make an effort to come up with multiple ideas.

4. Continue to revise your cards to include new ideas or improve on old ones. Then, from each subheading, choose the finest material.

You can now begin adding, deleting, and rewording your cards, as well as looking for methods to connect your topics. This is also where you may start planning your PowerPoint presentation. (However, don't start this stage too soon, or you'll have to redo a lot of your work.)

5. Create a final set of cards whenever you're satisfied with your work.

Don't put your full speech on the cards; instead, make a list of keywords to help you remember what you're going to say.

ALLOW TIME for your ideas to incubate while you're working on your presentation. During the creative process, incubation refers to when you aren't consciously thinking about your speech. When you give your ideas time to develop, you'll notice that the parts of your speech giving you trouble will fall into place. That's because your ideas, like chicks in their shells in a real-life incubator, are growing and evolving while you're busy making an omelette or watching a football game.

Focusing on your priorities

Every speech is unique, but successful speakers all adhere to a few key principles. Consider the following questions as you prepare your presentation:

- What is the demographic of your target market? Consider your audience's backgrounds and experiences, and make sure your content is appropriate. (A joke about something that happened in the 1960s, for example, would fall flat with a younger audience.) Also, consider how familiar your listeners are with your issue. Use language that kids will comprehend, but don't talk down to them. You might even wish to do a pre-event survey of certain members of your audience to find out what they hope to learn from you.
- What do you think an appropriate title for your speech should be? You came up with a working title for your talk earlier. It's now time to put the finishing touches on that title. Your title should appropriately reflect your content, and if you're giving a presentation at a conference, it should also correspond to the conference's theme. It should also be memorable, especially if you're vying with other presenters for attention during break-out sessions. Try out your title on your partner or pals to see if it works.

- What are the most important points you want to make? You should have one main theme you emphasise at the start, refer to throughout your presentation, and then return to the conclusion. Ensure you don't go off on too many tangents that aren't related to the main point. A successful presentation will concentrate on a few central themes rather than a dozen.
- What is the duration of your presentation? As you practice your speech, keep track of the time. If the conference organisers have set a stringent time constraint for you, make your speech five or ten minutes shorter to ensure you finish on time. If you're worried about running out of time, add an extra five or ten minutes of optional material to your discussion.
- How will you entice your audience to listen to you at the start of your presentation? It's critical to get your presentation off to a strong start. Start with an engaging narrative, a bit of comedy, or an unexpected statistic, for example. Watching TED speeches online and seeing how the speakers begin their presentations is an excellent method to gather ideas.
- What level of depth should you go into? You want to persuade your audience, but you don't want to overwhelm them with numbers. Keep your presentation basic and provide handouts with more extensive information if you want to provide many data and numbers.
- How can technical information be made more understandable? Check to see whether you can convey this information in various ways (for example, verbally and with a slide), and then summarise it before moving on to the next topic.

- How do you make your viewers picture the scenarios you're describing? Using the phrase "imagine" is an excellent technique to assist your reader's picture. For example, if you're discussing identity theft protection, say something like, "Imagine you go online today to check your bank account, and..." It's a void."

How do you ensure that you're providing the most accurate and up-to-date information possible? Searching the Internet for "best practices" is one approach to find out if your material is up to date — also to get terrific ideas for topics to include in your lecture. Make sure to insert the phrase "best practices" in quotation marks before listing your topic, like the following:

INVENTORY CONTROL "BEST PRACTICES"

How do you encourage them to buy in? If you're giving a compelling presentation, you'll only be successful if you can persuade your audience to agree with you. Consider the following questions:

- Why should folks care about what you've got to say?
- What problem can you help them with?
- What do you want them to do, and how will they be able to accomplish it?
- What are the advantages of doing what you're asking for them, their companies, or their families?
- Are there any associated costs or risks? If that's the case, how do the advantages outweigh the risks?
- What immediate action should they take, and why?

How can you spice up your presentation with visual aids? Visual aids are essential for any long presentation since they capture your audience's attention and help them remember crucial ideas. A boring or overly wordy PowerPoint, on the other hand, might easily lose your audience. If you don't know how to make PowerPoint presentations or other visual aids, ask the assistance of a friend or coworker who is.

How can you make a solid conclusion to your presentation? Consider how you might end your speech on a high note; for example, if you are giving a talk about personal development, you might end by saying, "You've all heard the famous quote, 'To be, or not to be: that is the question.' Today, I've given you some great ideas for how to 'be' and how to like that being inside you." You can also end with a call to action or a humorous remark if you have a strong rapport with your audience. Make it apparent that your chat is over, regardless of whatever option you take.

THERE's a lot more to give a talk than just talking! Even the best speech can be ruined if your audiovisual equipment isn't working, your space isn't set up correctly, or the air conditioner breaks down.

Make thorough arrangements ahead of time to help avoid surprises like this, which are especially damaging to introverts. Here are some of the details you should look into.

PREPARING **for a talk in your office**

If you're giving a presentation at work, the first thing you should do is reserve the room, which many people overlook. In most cases, people overlook this minor but crucial information.

Also, make sure you have all of the necessary audiovisual equipment. If you don't know how to use this equipment, ask your more tech-savvy coworkers for help — and make sure at least one of them can attend your presentation.

Finally, determine how you want your conference space to

be set up. Set up chairs on the right and left sides of the room with an aisle in between if there will be more than 20 guests. This layout will allow attendees to enter and exit the room easily, and if you're feeling brave, you can even walk up and down the aisle while speaking.

Preparing for a speech at a facility

If you're giving a presentation at a venue other than your own, make sure you work out all of the specifics with the venue or the talk's sponsors ahead of time. If you're presenting a keynote speech, for example, consider the following questions:

- If problems happen during your presentation, who can you contact at the facility?
- When you arrive at the venue, where can you park?
- How many people do you anticipate attending your speech?
- Who will be the one to introduce you?
- When and who else will be speaking at the event?

This last piece of information is critical because it allows you to refer to other people's presentations, which is a terrific way to build goodwill.

Also, mention the sort of microphone you want and, if applicable, the type of podium. Also, make sure you understand how to use any equipment you'll be using. Also, make sure you or the event site has backup equipment in case something goes wrong.

You'll need to make additional arrangements if you're conducting a lengthier seminar or workshop. Work with the facility to figure out how you want the space set up, what refreshments you want to be served, and when you want to take breaks, for example. If, for example, you find it easier to communicate when the illumination is lower, you may have unique lighting demands.

Practising your technique

You want to come across as clear, forceful, and compelling when you communicate. To do so, you must be at ease with your subject matter.

Start practising your speech aloud about a week ahead of time. Here's a seven-day strategy for getting ready for the big day. (You are free to change it to suit your needs.)

DAY 1:

For the first time, say your speech aloud. Make modifications since it will sound different when spoken aloud than it does on paper. Record your speech while you practice it, if possible. You'll naturally come up with good lead-ins, transitions, and phrasings as you speak. These thoughts can be transferred from your recording to your speech notes.

DAY 2:

Concentrate on the big picture.

Make a list of your primary points and the stories you'd like to convey.

Look for areas with weak transitions, drab writing, or a lack of "punch," and see if you can enliven them with proverbs, one-liners, quotes, and stories.

DAY 3:

Work on putting some personality into your work. Assume you're a politician, and add forcefulness, excitement, or even flamboyance to your delivery. Work on the following abilities to improve your public image:

- **Correct breathing:** As a speaker, correct breathing is the most crucial skill to master since it allows you to sound assertive and project your voice effectively. Place one hand on the top of your stomach, just below the ribs, to feel your diaphragm and practice right breathing. Inhale deeply through your nose, envisioning the air filling your stomach and flowing backwards. You should feel your diaphragm expand. When you exhale, your diaphragm should return to its original position. When you're breathing, your shoulders shouldn't move. This talent, by the way, will come in handy not just in public speaking but also in everyday life.
- **Changing the volume knob:** Nothing says "boring" like a monotone voice, so mix it up now and then. While you want to draw people's attention, get a little louder when you're making an important point, or get very quiet when you want to get people's attention.
- **Get moving:** The more you move, your voice moves, which helps you keep your listeners' attention.
- **Taking a quick pause before or after a vital point:** A brief pause will jolt your audience awake and ensure that they pay attention to your message.
- **When you make an important point, lean in close to your audience:** This trick exudes confidence and allows you to connect with your audience.
- **Mumbling:** Introverts tend to mumble. Practice standing up straight and projecting your voice to avoid this issue. The trick is to act as if there are extra rows behind the last row and project your voice to that row.

- **Pivoting:** Introverts frequently make the error of speaking to the screen behind them rather than to the people in front of them. Master the art of turning back to your audience, even when pointing to the screen, to avoid making this mistake. Even better, project our presentation onto a screen behind you as well as a laptop in front of you. You won't have to look at the screen behind you as often this way.

Day 4:

Practice with your props and audiovisual gear. Make a mark on your cards to indicate where your audiovisual assets will be used. Work on your walking to the podium and your motions.

Day 5:

Run through a dress rehearsal. Wear the same clothes you'll be wearing on the big day, and make full use of your props. Complete the entire run-through without pausing.

Day 6:

Deliver your speech in front of a small group of friends. Allow them to ask questions at the end of the presentation. Consider any last-minute adjustments you might be able to make.

Day 7:

Try the "whisper and speed-through" method. On the day of your presentation, whisper the first few minutes of your speech to yourself, then double-time the rest of it. Then, to loosen up your voice, say "Hey" a couple of times at full volume. Do a massive stretch like a lion after that. You're now ready to address your audience!

WHILE ALL OF this practice is essential, it's also critical to set aside some time to unwind. You can relieve stress by reading a book, watching a TV show, or spending time with friends or family.

20

Grabbing Your Audience: How To Win Them Over

PEOPLE UNDERSTAND that giving a speech is difficult, and they admire those who dare to do so. As a result, even before you begin speaking, your audience will be ready to love you. When you start chatting, here's how to make sure they stay on your side.

Making your listeners feel comfortable and connected

When you stand in front of an audience, people have high expectations of you. They want to be educated, entertained, persuaded, or challenged in some way. But do you know what they want? They want to know you're at ease since it will help them feel at ease as well.

So show your audience that you're at ease and excited. Act as if you're having a good time. It's important to remember that emotions are contagious! This is an excellent opportunity to employ some of the previously discussed pretend-extrovert body language. Lean in close to your audience, make large motions, and smile with your entire face.

Also, make it apparent that what you're expressing is something you believe in. If you're passionate about your subject, it will come over in your tone of voice and body language.

Also, keep in mind the pivot mentioned before in this chapter. Pivot your body at least somewhat toward your listeners when pointing to a slide behind you. You'll look less like you're talking to yourself and more like you're talking to them.

HERE ARE some more effective methods to engage with your listeners:

- Make meaningful eye contact with each audience member at least once if you're speaking to a small group. Before you talk, attempt to make eye contact with at least three of them.
- Use the "third eye" strategy if your audience is larger or making direct eye contact difficult. When looking at someone, direct your gaze to the area between their brows on their foreheads. It will appear to your listeners as though you are staring them in the eyes.
- Show that you care about your audience's well-being. If you think the room is excessively hot, for example, ask them: "Is it too hot in here for you?" If that's the case, request that the personnel lower the temperature.
- Make an honest effort to connect with your audience. For instance, you may honestly compliment them by saying something like, "It's wonderful to discuss this topic with people who are so knowledgeable about it."
- Bring your audience closer to you. The shorter the gap between you and them, the stronger the connection will be. If you're speaking on stage, for example, move to the very front of the stage.

- Make it clear to your audience what they may expect. For example, let them know how and when you'll manage queries and when you'll take breaks upfront.
- If you're speaking in front of a large gathering, make a point of repeating each question. You may ensure that everyone in the audience can hear it (especially those in the rear of the room) and that you heard it correctly yourself by doing so.
- When responding to questions, consider the person who asked the question and the rest of the audience. Avoid going off on tangents that only a few individuals in the room will be interested in. Before allowing someone to ask a second question, offer everyone an opportunity to ask one.
- If you don't know the solution to a question, say, "I don't know, but I'll look into it for you." This shows that you care about the audience member.
- Complete the task on time! Stop after you've said what you need to say — not everything you want to say.

Here's another piece of advice: stay in the moment. Don't just recite your speech word for word as you practised it. Instead, pay attention to how your audience reacts to your presentation. Keep an eye on them to see if they're interested, amused, offended, perplexed, or simply falling asleep. Keep doing what you're doing if they're still on board. However, if you're losing them, change the way you speak. Stop and ask questions if they are perplexed, for example. Take a little break if they're starting to fall off.

Also, make mental notes about the portions of your speech that need to be improved so you may edit them later. Another area where a skills coach might help is having trouble improving your material or presentation.

Finally, resist the temptation to apologise for any tiny

errors you may have made. This may cause your viewers to feel uneasy. It's also pointless because while you'll catch every mistake you make, your audience will miss the majority of them. So, if you make a mistake in a sentence, correct yourself and move on. However, if you make a major error, take a few moments to apologise and then return to your material.

Grabbing their attention with stories and humour

Dry figures and facts might support your arguments, but a compelling tale can make your message stick with your audience. Stories also serve another crucial function: they aid in the ice-breaking process between you and your audience.

Because stories are so effective, every world-class speaker incorporates them throughout their presentations. Of course, the trick is to choose the proper stories and present them well. Here are some pointers:

- Keep your story brief at the beginning so that the listeners aren't distracted by the intricacies. You can try lengthier stories if you've gotten more comfortable telling them.
- Concentrate on telling anecdotes that reinforce your main themes. Otherwise, you risk distracting your audience.
- Tell your personal stories. A few stories about your failings and foibles will help you appear modest and win over your audience. However, only share anecdotes like these if you're confident in your ability to come across as a confident presenter. They might make you look weak if you don't.
- Tell stories that appeal to the emotions of the audience.
- Tie the tale back to the point you wish to make in the end. "So the moral of the narrative is," for example.

When you're delivering a narrative, it's important to connect with your audience because it's similar to having a personal conversation. So go out from behind the podium, engage your audience, and employ some conversational gestures. Also, look for opportunities to use comedy, especially at the start of your presentation.

Although using comedy to connect with your audience is a terrific method to do so, do it with caution. Here are a few warnings:

- Make sure that everyone understands your joke.
- Stick to hilarious anecdotes or jokes that pertain to your topic throughout the body of your presentation. Off-topic comedy may garner a laugh, but it detracts from your message in the long run.
- To ensure that your stories or jokes do not insult anyone, think about them from every viewpoint. Also, even if your pals think they're funny, avoid any jokes that are even vaguely off-colour.
- Puns and groaners should be avoided. One lousy joke may be OK, but two or more could permanently alienate your audience.
- Talking to the people you meet daily is one of the best ways to develop funny stories.

Persuading with power

One of the most difficult speeches to deliver is a convincing speech because you must persuade a group of people who may be apathetic, indecisive, or even hostile.

The most common error presenters make in this type of presentation is to employ a hard sell. Your listeners are likely to protest if you twist their arms. And if you try to persuade them by instilling dread in them, your words will be ineffective.

Smart persuaders, on the other hand, concentrate on two skills: matching and timing.

UNDERSTANDING MATCHING **and pacing**

Matching and pacing are two of the most powerful tools in a speaker's repertoire. They can even make the difference between a great speech and a disaster.

Matching is built on the idea that to encourage others to change, you must first see things from their perspective. Consider this: I think a flower is pink, but Tom thinks it's orange. I can hammer Tom with facts and opinions all day, but the chances are he'll just respond with his facts and ideas. And at some point, he'll simply shut down.

Instead, if I'm smart, I'll utilise matching. I'm going to put myself in Tom's position and try to figure out why he thinks the bloom is orange. This does not imply that I must concur with him. But it means I'll have to consider the flower from Tom's point of view.

Instead of coming across as a critical person who thinks, "I need to enlighten Tom about his delusion," I'll come across as an ally who is interested in his ideas and opinions when I do this.

Similarly, if you're trying to persuade a whole audience to change, you must first understand where they're coming from. For example, if you're trying to persuade a group of individuals to consider a new phone system, consider the following:

- What features of their present phone system do these people appreciate?
- Is it possible that they have valid reasons for resisting change?
- Are they likely to consider both the benefits and the additional expenses associated with a new system?

With this knowledge, you may demonstrate to your audience that you understand their situation. After that, you can begin gently moving them to your position using a technique known as pacing.

Identifying the five stages of a persuasive talk

You must win over your listeners in phases to obtain their attention, trust, and buy-in. Here are five steps to help you get started.

1. Create awareness

You want to use matching in your introduction to demonstrate to your audience that you understand their predicament. Furthermore, you should characterise the subject you're discussing and explain it in a way that engages your audience. Finally, it would be best to persuade them that you are an expert deserving of their time and attention.

Are you attempting to persuade your audience to use a new and more secure sort of banking software, for example? If that's the case, put the following in your opening:

- Give an example of a hacker taking down a bank's entire system to let your audience understand the danger they're in. Then, provide data on the cost of internet theft.
- Mention one or two reasons why your audience might be hesitant to acquire your new system to demonstrate that you understand their concerns. Recognise that funds are tight and that they might not want to spend the money. (That's matching.) Then reassure them by telling them that you'll address their worry during your presentation.
- Establish your credibility to show your audience why they should listen to you. You're expecting people to change, which makes them nervous — so

demonstrate that you're someone they can rely on to lead them in the right direction—lay out your credentials and share real-life experiences about your expertise with banking systems to accomplish this.

If you achieve this step, your audience will think to themselves, "This individual knows what he's talking about." This is the first stage of persuasion.

2. Describe the problem in detail.

Expand on the topic you want your audience to think about in your first main point. Would you mind providing them with concrete information on how the issue affects them today and how it is likely to affect them, their family, or their firm in the future?

Avoid making blanket statements like, "If you don't upgrade your system, you'll be attacked within the year." Instead, say something more cautious like, "I have severe worries that your existing system is leaving you vulnerable to an assault shortly, and here's why."

Would you mind continuing to show your listeners that you understand and empathise with their predicament? Say something like, "It's irritating when that happens, isn't it?" or "It's frustrating when that happens, isn't it?" or "Isn't it true that when this problem arises, it throws your entire enterprise into disarray?"

You want your audience to think at the end of this stage, "He knows our stance, and we understand his." And he's not simply trying to sell us anything. We can see why he thinks this is such a crucial problem for us."

3. Use pace to describe the answer.

Tell your listeners how they can solve their problem in

your second main point. This is when you'll start pacing or moving your viewers from their perspective to yours.

Begin by discussing all conceivable answers, then focus on the best one (which is, of course, the one you're proposing). Be truthful while doing so. List the advantages and disadvantages of each option, including the one you prefer. You will gain the trust of your audience if you do so.

At this point, your goal is to foster a collaborative mindset. When you do, your audience will think to themselves, "Of all the options, this is the best."

4. Encourage your audience to imagine themselves succeeding

Encourage your audience to actively see themselves addressing their problem in your third main point. As a result, the solution will feel more real to them.

For instance, say something like this:

"Imagine you're employing this technology right now on your nursing floors. Take a look at what the nurses are doing. Can you see how technology could make their work easier while saving you time and money? Will it provide you with improved readouts that will help you provide better care to your patients?

"Imagine if our firm took care of all of your time-consuming bookkeeping responsibilities. Furthermore, we ensure that your financial reports are compliant with all federal and state laws, so you don't have to worry about making costly mistakes. And we do it all at a price that is well within your means."

Also, include your audience in fun. Allow time for questions and comments, and ask your audience to imagine how they would use your product or service. You may transform your talk into a brainstorming session at this point, and your audience may come up with fantastic ideas that you hadn't even considered!

Finally, if possible, show a product, service, or expertise in action. This is an effective approach to gain the attention of your audience.

If you nail this step, your audience will say, "I understand how we can handle this problem or issue, and this is the method to accomplish it." You're almost there, but there's one more step to obtain full buy-in.

5. Make a plan of action.

As you near the end of your presentation, outline the steps your audience can take to achieve the goal you've suggested. Break these tasks down into small, manageable steps. Inquire if your audience has any questions about these activities, and make sure any misunderstandings are cleared up.

If you succeed in this step, your audience will say things like "I want to do this" and "How can I participate?" Then you can exclaim, "Hooray!" because you've completed your task!

CHANGING things up to keep your listeners' attention

Your audience has a short attention span, and if you lecture them for too long during a workshop or seminar, they will quickly fall asleep. The usual guideline is that you shouldn't go more than 30 minutes without doing something to break up the monotony.

To provide a change of pace for your listeners, you might offer a variety of activities. Ask your audience to participate in problem-solving exercises or have many people role-play an issue. You may even be able to pass artefacts around the room for your audience to inspect, depending on your topic.

Find strategies to appeal to each of the three types of learners:

- Lectures and question-and-answer sessions appeal to auditory learners.
- Visual learners appreciate handouts, PowerPoint presentations, and slide shows.
- Kinaesthetic learners enjoy action, so enlist their help by filling out paperwork or even moving around the room.

Handling hecklers with ease

If you're lucky, everyone in your audience will be friendly and sympathetic. However, there's always the possibility that you'll run into some nasty or obnoxious folks. If you're an extrovert, you can usually shake them off easily, but if you're an introvert, a heckler can completely derail your speech.

If you're being heckled, another powerful strategy is to maintain strong eye contact. As a result, your audience (and your heckler) will perceive you as assertive.

If someone mocks you, repeat the question so that everyone in the room hears it. Also, make sure you know exactly what the person is complaining about so you can respond appropriately. You might not have explained your argument well enough. If this is the case, you may apologise and restate your facts.

Also, try rephrasing the person's question in a more positive light. For example, if someone exclaims, "You're entirely wrong about that," calmly react with, "It's fascinating that you feel strongly about that subject." Many people do, so let me take a moment to lay out the information that led me to my conclusions." Also, look for areas where you and your partner agree. This will make the person more receptive to your message.

If a heckler isn't satisfied with your response and the rest of your audience wants to move on, you can offer to continue talking with the person after your speech. In rare circumstances, it may be more appropriate to say, "Let's agree to disagree simply." If you pick this option, be precise about the topic on which you disagree.

If you're heckled, keep in mind that the audience will usually turn against the heckler and want to protect you. So, if you just hold your cool, your listeners will develop a stronger bond with you than they did before the heckling.

Being yourself

Now that you know the guidelines for attracting your audience's attention, here's a bonus tip: if it works for you, feel free to break them.

Why? Because one rule takes precedence over all others: be loyal to yourself. When you're not pretending to be someone you're not, you'll be more calm and authoritative, and your audience will appreciate your honesty.

So, stick to the basic guidelines of public speaking, but add your flair to them. Just make sure you're still reaching out to your audience and conveying your message.

21

Dating Advice For Introverts

Is it important to you to find someone to love? Or are you in a relationship that you wish to strengthen and make more enjoyable? In any case, you'll find a lot of useful information in this chapter.

Dating can be thrilling, irritating, enjoyable, dull, or any combination of these emotions. But one thing is certain: it's a lot of work! You have to kiss a lot of frogs before you find a prince, as the adage goes (or princess). All that frog-kissing might be exhausting for introverts in particular.

Spotting people, you'd like to date

If you're unsure where to start looking for a soul mate, give that chapter a quick browse if you're unsure where to start.

In addition to these physical locations, introverts have another fantastic option for finding love: online dating sites. If you're an innie, these sites provide a lot of advantages, including the following:

- They allow you to learn more about someone before meeting them face to face, making it much easier to strike up a discussion when you do meet.

- They assist you in determining whether a possible date is introverted or extroverted. Extroverts, for example, prefer to jump right into a phone call or a date after exchanging a few e-mails. On the other hand, introverts like to exchange more e-mails and make one or two phone calls before committing to a face-to-face meeting.
- They can often tell you right away if you're compatible with someone, saving you from an embarrassing evening if you're not.
- If a date doesn't work out, there's a good chance you won't see the person again. As a result, it's less stressful than going on a horrible date with someone you see every day at work or in your apartment complex.

True, there are dangers associated with internet dating. You probably already know this as an introvert with a keen sense of danger, but just in case, here are a few reminders:

- Do not provide your e-mail address to an internet contact. Create a generic e-mail account that does not include your last name if you want to communicate outside of the dating service's site.
- Give the person your cellphone number, not your home phone number, if you want to exchange calls.
- Make sure your first two or three dates take place in a public place and let others know where you're going and when you'll be back.

Here are some more pointers on how to succeed in online dating:

- Start a conversation with only one person at a time. When you start a live chat or accept an

invitation to chat, only to disappear because you're chatting with someone else, it irritates other people.
- Treat the discussion as if it were a phone call. Don't just leave the conversation if you need to terminate it. Instead, say something along the lines of "Oops!" I need to sign off since something has just come up. "I'm sorry," you say, and if you like the person and want to talk more, you say so.
- Consider conducting the "dump sheet" about your first phone conversation if you're worried about your nervousness getting in the way. This practice will assist you in de-stressing and overcoming your worries. Also, when you're on the phone, it's fine to admit that you're nervous. State, "I'm new to this whole thing, and I'm not sure how it works." People will most likely be understanding — and if they aren't, they aren't a good match for you anyhow.
- Sending out "form letter" e-mails to many people at once is not a good idea. (Others will notice if you do this and will hold it against you, possibly blocking your account and filing a complaint with the website.)
- Fill out at least half of the dating service's profile form. The majority of the inquiries they ask are harmless. If you're worried about answering them, Internet dating is probably not for you.

Making a first date work

Is there anything more nerve-wracking than going on a first date? Most likely not, particularly if you're an introvert. You might be stumped after saying "hi." What's the solution? Take a look at these suggestions:

- Before setting up a date, try to get to know the person over the phone. If you do, you'll have a good idea if the two of you would get along, and you'll know enough about the other person to come up with some conversation starters.
- Consider alternatives to a restaurant date because a small chat can be draining during a long meal. Instead, propose something else to do, like coffee or another activity. "Would you want to meet for coffee or supper — or do you ice skate?" is a good way to suggest something other than dinner. Do you? Then how about going ice skating?"
- Choose an event that has a set end time. If you know roughly how long your date will last, you'll feel more at ease.
- Take it easy on the booze. Set a clear limit for yourself if you're in an environment where alcohol is served. One glass of wine may help you relax and converse more readily, but three or four may cause you to do or say things you'll later regret.

Addressing expectations

If you're an introvert, you prefer to cultivate relationships over time. It's usually not a problem when you're dating another innie. When you're on a date with an extrovert, though, you and your date may have conflicting expectations about what will happen next.

Outies are frequently ready to get right into hugs and kisses (and more), whereas innies are still getting warmed up. As a result, extroverts may believe they are being ignored, while introverts may feel compelled to move too rapidly. And this can quickly suffocate a blossoming relationship.

Here are a few helpful tips for avoiding this issue:

- Carefully consider the timing and location of your first few dates. For example, instead of a romantic supper, suggest a daytime baseball game for your first date, and make it clear that you have another commitment later that day. This will indicate that you are not looking to get intimate right soon.
- Make public adulation for them. If your supervisor compliments you at a meeting, say something like, "Thank you, I appreciate it." In turn, I'd like to express my gratitude to Jack, who made it possible for us to complete the project on time."
- Consider how you may assist them by recognising their requirements. Is there a lot of pressure on them? You might be able to help them out with their initiatives. Is there a new technology that they're having trouble with that you've mastered? Then you can pitch in with your knowledge.
- Instantly respond to their e-mails and phone calls. You'll be demonstrating your respect for them if you do so.
- Go above and above if you're working together on a project. You'll be remembered if you go above and beyond what they expect.
- Make a list of reasons why you want to talk to them. For instance, if you observe that a coworker is having problems with a new software application you've mastered, offer to buy her lunch and pick her brain about the new accounting system she's made, or offer to let her pick your brain about the new accounting system she's created. By the time you get to dessert, you'll have a new ally if all goes well.
- Volunteer to help at charity events hosted by your employer. Volunteering lets others know right away that you're a good person. Therefore you'll have an advantage right away.

- Maintain contact with your new allies. Stop by their offices now and then to speak, stay up to date on their initiatives, and invite them to lunch. You'll strengthen the bonds you've created by doing so.
- Make your expectations clear when you're ready for intimacy. Let your date know if you're prepared for kissing and cuddling but not for anything more. For instance, you could remark, "I'm a little old-fashioned, and I prefer to take things slowly." However, if you're ready to take your relationship to the next level, make sure your words and body language reflect your feelings. (Sexy music and candles can also send a strong message!)
- Open up emotionally to the other person while you're getting serious. Introverts are generally hesitant to express "I love you," whereas extroverts (like introverts) require these words. So, if you're ready to commit to a serious relationship, say those three words – it's not as difficult as you would think!

Enjoying a Deep and Healthy Relationship

When you're casually dating, getting along is usually very simple. When you share a house and a bed, though, things grow a lot more complicated. As a result, you'll have to work harder to maintain your connection strong.

GRASPING **the basics of a good relationship**

A healthy relationship involves the three Ls: like, love, and lust. And that is an excellent list! You have all the essentials in place if you sincerely enjoy the other person as a friend, have a deep affection for them, and have wonderful chemistry with them. Don't worry if it takes time for love or friendship to bloom or chemistry to kick in if two out of three is a decent start — or perhaps enough. (However, if that doesn't happen over time, consider whether you require more.)

Couples are more likely to succeed if they have two other factors working in their favour: mutual respect and mutual trust. These are, in fact, "musts" for a successful relationship, in my opinion.

However, feelings alone aren't enough to keep a relationship alive. It's also crucial to translate your emotions into actions. These are the seven principles of a healthy relationship, according to him:

1. CREATING MENTAL "LOVE MAPS" in which you store knowledge about your partner's dreams, hopes, fears, and feelings to understand them better.

Your love map, for example, might look like this:

- As a therapist, John is passionate about making the world a safer place for the children he works with.
- He fantasies about us having a large family of our own.
- He's worried that he won't be able to live up to his parent's expectations.
- He appears assertive on the outside, but he is uneasy on the inside and has difficulty expressing his demands.

2. Nurturing your feelings for and admiration for your partner, as well as recognising the reality that they are not the same as you.

3. Turning toward your spouse rather than away; in other words, rather than brushing off your partner's attempts to

develop physical or verbal connections with you, respond favourably to them.

4. Allowing your partner to influence you by letting go of the belief that you are always correct and allowing yourself to be influenced by your partner's views.

5. Collaboration to tackle any challenges that can be solved

6. Even if you can't solve a situation, empathising with your partner's point of view

7. Establishing family traditions, for example, might help to create shared meaning.

AND THERE's one more factor that's critical for a good relationship: shared core values. Successful marriages, for example, may share the following values:

- We both believe that financial stability is a priority.
- We both believe that lifelong learning is critical.
- We both place a high priority on staying in shape.

SHARED ideals lead to shared behaviours, which help to strengthen a bond. If you both value fitness, for example, you'll encourage each other to work out and eat healthily. If you both agree that financial security is essential for a happy life, you'll both make wise financial decisions. You'll like sharing everything from museum excursions to martial arts courses if you both embrace lifelong learning. As a result, instead of thinking, "He's a jerk," you'll enjoy each other's company and sincerely respect your partner.

On the other side, if your core values differ from your partner's, getting along can be challenging.

It can be a deal-breaker if your partner doesn't share your core values, depending on how strong they are. As a result, it's critical to discuss these principles early on in your relationship.

Recognising how different personalities mesh in relationships

Understanding the ground principles for a good relationship is crucial, considering how different personalities might affect that relationship. As you might expect, one of the most intriguing factors to explore is whether each member of a partnership is introverted or extroverted.

People frequently believe that partners with similar personalities will get along the best. However, according to one study, the opposite is generally true in the long run. The researchers polled 67 couples, all of whom were in their forties or older, about how happy they were in their marriages. They discovered that couples with highly comparable introversion or extroversion ratings were less satisfied in middle age than couples with less similar values.

Why? Couples with different interests and abilities may find it easier to divide tasks, according to the experts. An extroverted partner, for example, may be better at coaching kids' soccer games or resolving neighbour disputes, whereas an introverted partner may be better at keeping the chequebook straight and assisting the kids with homework.

Another study, on the other hand, reveals that pairing an extroverted woman with an introverted male might sometimes result in additional conflict. One reason, according to the researchers, is that this pairing is unusual in many cultures. Many introverted men and extroverted women couples and many innie-innie and outie-outie relationships work out well.

We've all met happy bookish couples and outgoing couples that travel and party all the time.

What's the bottom line? Whether you're both introverts, both extroverts, or an innie-outie mix, you and your partner are likely to be happy if you respect each other's needs and embrace the key principles.

HANDLING INNIE-OUTIE DIFFERENCES Successfully

Introvert-extrovert couples, according to the study, have a good chance of attaining long-term happiness together. Their disparate personalities, on the other hand, might make life difficult at times. If you and your spouse are in an innie-outie relationship, here are some ways to keep you and your partner satisfied and happy.

Identifying each other's requirements and passions

People who are in relationships frequently expect their partners to read their minds. Even the closest of partners, though, often have no idea what's going on in each other's heads, particularly at the beginning of a relationship when people are still getting to know one another. "When it comes to excellent relationships, there is no such thing as ESP.

If you're an introvert in a relationship with an extrovert, your partner demands special consideration. Most likely, you find it difficult to express your sentiments, especially in the early stages of a relationship. As a result, your loved one is likely to be completely unaware of your preferences and requirements. This is aggravating for your outie and can result in the following issues:

- Your partner may make incorrect assumptions about your needs and desires to "fill in the blanks."
- Your partner may stop soliciting your opinion and begin making decisions without consulting you.

- Because you aren't contributing your thoughts and opinions, your partner may become more demanding and overbearing.
- Your extroverted partner, on the other hand, may talk about his hobbies and expectations regularly. And you could conclude, "All he talks about is himself." "How about myself?"

If that's the case, you might be surprised to learn that your outie partner doesn't always want to be in charge. From his perspective, you're creating a void that he must fill.

Fortunately, there is a simple solution to this problem. But here's the thing: if you're in a relationship with an introvert, the ball is in your court. That's because you're the one who's keeping important information hidden.

So, even if it makes you uncomfortable, open up. Let your partner know what you enjoy, dislike, and what you hope to get out of your life and relationship. Allow him to share this information with you as well.

This is a good way to start the discussion. Choose a quiet period and ask each of you to answer the following questions:

- What does a great vacation look like to you? Isn't this the ideal weekend?
- What is your most essential career goal?
- What is the most pressing issue you wish to address in your life?
- What would you do with an extra hour each day if you had it?
- What aspect of your future concerns you the most? What aspect of your future excites you the most?

Also, be open about your past experiences. Investigating your partner's early years can help you better grasp his current wants and ambitions. For example, you may discover that your partner is hesitant to have children because he grew up in an abusive household and fears that he will not be a good father. If that's the case, you'll be able to handle the situation with tact and empathy.

FIGURING out how to talk with each other

Introverts and extroverts appear to speak different languages at times. In some ways, they do! That's because they communicate in completely different ways, which can get them into many difficulties. Here are some of the issues that frequently arise when innie-outie couples converse:

- The extrovert may jump from topic to topic quickly, denying the introvert the opportunity to ponder about each one.
- The introvert may listen calmly and without displaying emotion, giving the impression that she is bored to the extrovert.
- The extrovert may become overly enthusiastic about the conversation, interrupting the introvert, who needs time to think about what she wants to say.
- The introvert may shut out the extrovert's small talk, causing him to become irritated when he sees she isn't paying attention.
- While the introvert ponders, "Will she ever shut up and let me talk about something more interesting?" the extrovert wonders, "Will she ever shut up and let me talk about something more interesting?" (Of course, other introverts who aren't interested in that issue will feel the same way!)
- The extrovert may get home from work or school brimming with stories from the day, whereas the introvert may require some quiet time to relax before engaging in conversation.
- Extroverts may overcompensate for an introvert's

quiet by chatting excessively to fill the void. When this occurs, the introvert may become resentful of or overwhelmed by the extrovert's constant chatter.

Fortunately, there are ways for you and your partner to communicate on the same page. If you're the introvert in your relationship, here are some helpful hints:

When it comes to small conversation, give your outie partner a chance. To him, it's like food and oxygen, so act as though you're interested even if you aren't!

Allow your interest to show on your face and in your voice when an extrovert is speaking. "No way – he did that?" you might express enthusiasm with phrases like "No way — he did that?" or "Wow, that's incredible!"

Be honest but empathetic if your partner is eager to share his news, but you need some time to recharge your battery before a long talk. For instance, you could respond, "I'd like to hear more about that." But, if you could give me a few minutes to clear my thoughts and get dinner started, that would be great. Then we can have a glass of wine, and you can tell me everything."

Keep an eye on your partner's body language when you're talking about one of your favourite topics. If he appears perplexed, write down some of your thoughts for him. If he appears bored, though, try ending the conversation and moving on to a different topic.

Extroverts are known for being "big picture" thinkers. Focus on your main ideas unless it's necessary to give your outie partner many specifics.

Assist your extroverted spouse in better understanding how to communicate with you. Try the following:

- Request that he speak more slowly so that you can understand what he's saying.
- If he has a habit of interrupting you, tell him you need a few moments to finish your thought before

he jumps in. (And be gentle with him as he overcomes his want to butt in; it takes time to break a bad habit.)
- If he can't stop talking at a million miles per hour, gradually slow him down by asking for examples. If he's a teacher, for example, and he's complaining about the school's new maths syllabus, ask him to describe some of the problems with it to you.
- Also, as the two of you grow closer, see if you can both focus on matching and pacing during discussions, which means talking at a comparable speed and emotional intensity.
- When one of you is upset, emotional "matching" is extremely crucial. Imagine calling a company and stating, "The vacuum cleaner I got from you yesterday just caught fire!" and get an "Oh, yes" as a response. I see your point. But just take it easy."
- Instead, attempt to respond with enough emotion in the circumstances like this to convey that you're worried and empathic. As a result, your partner will feel listened to and will be able to control his own emotions.

Looking for win-win solutions

There will be challenges to work through in any relationship. It's even more difficult to deal with these challenges if you and your partner have extremely different personalities. To be successful in discovering answers, the two of you must begin as allies rather than adversaries.

When you're on opposing sides of an issue, remember that the goal isn't for you to "win" while your spouse "ends up losing." Instead, look for solutions that benefit both of you. Here's how to go about it:

1. Make a list of all the areas where you agree and write them down.

2. Identify the places where you disagree.
   Frequently, you'll discover that what appears to be a major disagreement is a little one.

3. Look for any evidence of progress in your conversation, even if they are minor. When you make headway toward an agreement, reinforce each other positively with a kind comment, a hug, or a "thank you."

4. Recognise that you and your partner may tackle things differently.

INTROVERTS ARE MORE likely to focus on the half-empty glass, whereas extroverts are more likely to focus on what is going well. As a result, an innie may be overly pessimistic when it comes to solving a problem, whereas an outie may gloss over significant concerns. It will be easier for you both to meet in the middle if you are both aware of this.

When arranging social activities, seek win-win solutions in particular. You have the right as an innie to say no to an overflowing social calendar. On the other hand, your extroverted partner has the right to recharge his batteries by socialising with others. So, while you're planning your social calendar, sit down together and ask questions like these:

- How many obligations do you and your partner already have?
- What forthcoming social engagements do your

extroverted partner consider "must attend" activities?
- Is that a list you can handle? If not, will your partner be able to attend some occasions without you?
- Can you commit to having at least a couple of discussions with people when you do go to gatherings together, rather than just sitting in a corner or watching TV?
- When can you get together for some quiet, intimate time to address your needs?

When you eventually agree on your social obligations, you'll probably only get half of what you desire. But you'll both get what you want: a chance to recharge your batteries in your unique way.

Identifying the real source of your issues

It would help if you went to the root of a problem to solve it successfully. And occasionally, the problems you attribute to your introvert-extrovert differences are caused by something else entirely.

For one thing, adults frequently pick up views and habits from their own families without even realising it. If your father cursed like a pirate while your partner's father never said anything more than "drat," the two of you may have quite different perspectives on whether or not cursing is acceptable in your home. Those ideas will most likely have little to do with your personality and everything to do with your upbringing. One reason for this is that sharing information about your families and childhoods might make it easier to appreciate and respect your differences.

Furthermore, problems attributed to personality conflicts might occasionally indicate something more serious: a mental condition. You may be coping with one of these issues if your relationship is severely difficult — or if either of you exhibits troubling or unsettling behaviours:

- Depression.
- An anxiety disorder.
- Attention deficit hyperactivity disorder (ADHD) or attention deficit disorder (ADD).
- A personality disorder.
- Post-traumatic stress disorder (PTSD).
- A problem with drugs or alcohol.
- An eating disorder.

Consult a psychologist or a psychiatrist if you feel that any of these concerns are causing problems in your relationship. A proper diagnosis and treatment can make all the difference in the world!

SPLITTING UP SANELY

There must be 50 ways to leave your beloved, as the song goes, but that doesn't mean it's ever simple to break up. A breakup, whether you're the one saying goodbye or the one who gets rejected, can be an extremely terrible event.

If you're an introvert, a breakup might be extra painful since you put so much of yourself into each of your relationships. You're also prone to blaming yourself when things go wrong. As a result, you may find yourself wondering what went wrong for days or weeks when a relationship ends. (Extroverts may also blame themselves, but they tend to recover faster.)

Fortunately, you can make a breakup less painful for both you and your ex. Doing the activities outlined in the last chapter for combating negative self-talk is one good technique. Also, take a look at the suggestions in the following areas.

When you're getting dumped

If your lover is the one who is breaking up with you, handle the situation as follows:

- Refrain from pleading with the person to stay. The relationship is ended if your partner says it is.
- Avoid placing blame on yourself or your partner. Humans aren't perfect, and you've probably both made mistakes. If you're stuck in a cycle of self-blame, try the dump sheet and other activities.
- Find a way to express your feelings. You may find it tough to discuss a breakup with your friends and family if you are an introvert. So express yourself through journaling, drawing, or music, or using a sport like kickboxing or tennis to take out your hurt and fury physically.
- Recognise that getting over a breakup takes time. You'll go through the usual grief cycle of denial, anger, bargaining, melancholy, and acceptance if your partner bids farewell.

When this happens, keep in mind that your emotions may not always follow this neat pattern. They could emerge in any sequence, in rapid succession, or even all at the same moment. Even if you think you've moved past one stage of the cycle, it's possible to fall back into it. Allow yourself time to finish this process, and remember that it's a normal and healthy way to get back on your feet.

Even after a heartbreaking breakup, you're likely to find yourself "whitewashing" the situation — that is, saying things like, "It's all for the best that we've split up." While whitewashing can be problematic in some situations, it's a perfectly acceptable response in this case if it helps you move on. It's preferable to dwell on the breakup or nursing a grudge, which can keep you locked in your current situation.

. . .

When you're doing the dumping

If you're the one who's breaking up with someone, follow these steps:

- Make sure you truly want to end your relationship. Allow yourself several days to calm down and mull things through rationally if you've just disagreed. Also, be aware that introverts may withdraw their best supporters in the face of personal troubles or catastrophes. Check to see if you're making the same error.
- Wait for the perfect opportunity. Avoid stating "it's over" in the middle of a fight, and don't catch your partner off guard during a pleasant moment. Instead, choose a time when you are both relaxed and tranquil. And if your relationship has been going on for more than a month or two, don't split up with a text message or an e-mail! Even if breaking up in person is unpleasant, it demonstrates respect for the other person, which will be appreciated.
- Choose the appropriate location. In general, it's preferable to make your goals known in secret rather than in public. If you're scared, the other person may become aggressive or even violent; meet in a public place with easy exits and bring a friend or two with you.
- Expect some repercussions. Your girlfriend is likely to be hurt or angry if she isn't ready to end the relationship. As a result, she might say something hurtful. Maintain your composure and allow her to vent without retaliating.
- Don't give up. Stick to your decision once you've made it.

It may be simple to get your life back on track if you're

breaking up after a brief romance. If you're leaving a serious, long-term relationship, though, it might be a good idea to seek counselling. A qualified therapist can help you get through any remaining anger or self-doubt so you can join a new, healthy relationship with confidence.

22

What If Your Child Is An Introvert

DO YOU HAVE AN INTROVERTED CHILD? If that's the case, you're in for a wild ride! Your amazing youngster will most certainly amaze, frustrate, baffle, impress, and please you all at once. Introverted children are a joy to nurture, but they can also put your parenting skills to the test.

Introverted children are similar to introverted adults in many respects. If you think your child is an innie, the previous chapters can assist you in figuring out if you're correct. By simply watching your child, you can deduce a lot about their personality. If any of the following statements apply to your child, he or she is likely an innie:

- Before participating in an activity, your youngster observes other children from the sidelines for a long time.
- Your child can constantly chat about her interests with family and close friends, but she clams up in a group.
- Your child is wary of trying new things and is hesitant to do so.
- "She's so brilliant and talented, yet she won't speak up in class," your child's teacher says.

- Your youngster can concentrate on an activity or a book for hours.
- Your child spends a lot of time alone in her room, which she enjoys.
- At large social gatherings, your youngster tends to zone out or even go into meltdown.
- At school or on social occasions, your child's body language is "silent," yet at home, her motions may be quite lively.
- Your child has a tiny circle of friends, and she may wield a lot of power inside that circle.
- Before she speaks, your youngster should ponder.
- If you have a lot of after-school or weekend activities planned for your child, she will be upset.
- Your youngster would rather not be the focus of attention.
- Your child may create the impression to other children that she is "stuck up."
- Your youngster favours muted hues that help her to blend in rather than bright colours.
- Your child prefers to work on school projects by himself rather than in a group.

Many young innies, like introverted adults, are labelled as shy (for more on shyness, and many children are both shy and introverted). However, many innie children aren't shy; they just prefer little doses of socialising since they recharge their batteries by turning inside rather than outward.

Some introverted children (but not all) are also highly sensitive. Sights, smells, noises, tastes, textures, emotions, and physical pain can all trigger significant reactions in these youngsters.

Creating an Innie-Friendly Home for Your Child

In the outside world, introverted youngsters face various problems, including crowded classrooms, noisy birthday celebrations, and even encounters with schoolyard bullies. So having a caring, understanding family and an innie-friendly environment where they can rest, feel appreciated, and replenish their batteries is vital for them. In this section, discuss how to make your child's home life comfortable and enjoyable.

APPRECIATING your child's innie-ness

The first step in providing a good home for an innie child is to examine your soul. Why? Because accepting your child as she is is the first step toward her happiness as an introvert.

If you're an extrovert, you might find it challenging to comprehend how your introverted child thinks and acts. But it's critical to understand that her way of life isn't wrong; it's simply different.

As a result, be careful not to place unreasonable expectations on your child. Instead of being a social butterfly, she'll most likely make a few close friends. Allow her the quiet time she requires to refill her batteries and be understanding if she seems overwhelmed by activities you enjoyed as a kid.

What if you're a self-described introvert? On the one hand, you'll be able to comprehend your child's perspective. On the other hand, you may reflect on your difficulties as a child and project your emotional baggage onto your child. Recognise that your child isn't you if you catch yourself doing this. She'll face some of the same issues you faced as an introvert, but she'll deal with them differently. As a result, take care to keep your emotions distinct from hers.

Avoid the urge to try to change your child's personality, whether you're an introverted or extroverted parent.

It's a bad idea to push an innie to become more extroverted. Your child may choose to develop some outie behaviours on her own at some point in the future, but it must be her decision. And if she decides she'd rather be a full-fledged innie, that's a perfectly acceptable option as well.

However, make it clear to your little introvert that you expect her to be a family member. Make your expectations clear on this front; for example, tell her you to expect her to join the family for dinner every night. Set rules for family activities early on, stick to them (though you can alter them as your child grows older), and model them for your child.

STEERING clear of the over-scheduling trap

Today's children typically have schedules that are even busier than their parents. They could range from playdates to football practice to music courses, for example. That's fantastic if the children are high-energy extroverts who enjoy flitting from one activity to the next. However, for introverted children, such a schedule can be extremely stressful and result in meltdowns.

To replenish their batteries, young innies must retreat within. So take a break from your child! Introduce your innie to new experiences, but do so in a way that does not overwhelm her. Here are some suggestions:

- Choose only one activity at a time if your introvert is very young, and allow her to ease into it gradually. If you sign up your 4-year-old for a tap dance class, for example, ask the teacher if it's okay for him or her to sit quietly on the sidelines for the first session (unless she wants to join in). Allow her to gradually increase her participation over the next few sessions at her speed.
- Allow your child to explore the hobbies she enjoys rather than pressuring her to continue with something she doesn't enjoy. Allow her to grow

gently when she attempts a new activity, and praise her for taking modest steps.
- Avoid arranging tasks that are too close together. Make sure your child gets some quiet downtime after each activity so she can recuperate. Allow your child to say no if something is too much for her, such as when a coach says, "We're all going out for pizza after the match."
- Consider enrolling your youngster in the same activity twice. She might love it a lot more the second time around, given that she knows what to expect.
- Give your child a variety of activities to choose from. She will be more willing to try something new if she has a choice.
- Allow your older child or teen to determine the pace when it comes to extracurricular activities if you're a parent. Respect her interests and provide her with the supplies she needs to continue her hobbies if she enjoys activities she does alone, such as painting or playing the violin.
- Avoid falling into the trap of believing that your child must partake in the activities that you enjoyed as a youngster (especially if you're an extrovert).

Whether you're organising activities for a younger or older innie, keep in mind that separating from their parents or leaving their homes for extended periods can be tough for these children. Separation anxiety is more common in quiet toddlers than in their outie peers, while older children and teens may become anxious if they have to go away to summer camp or attend an out-of-town band concert.

Prepare your innie kids ahead of time to make these times easier for them. If you're enrolling your child in a gymnastics class, for example, take her to the facility ahead of time and show her images of other children participating in gymnastics, so she knows what to expect. Show older innie flyers about the camp and describe the activities she'll be doing if she's worried about going to camp.

Above all, make your child's first social interactions with others as positive as possible. A persistently overstimulated young innie may become even more hesitant to explore new things. In addition, an introverted youngster who is forced into demanding social activities that she is not ready for may fail and develop frightened of social situations in the future. So plan and organise activities that don't put too much pressure on your quiet child.

Helping your innie child handle change

Extroverted children are used to dealing with change, but unpredictability can be overwhelming for early innies. However, because life is full of shocks and changes, it's critical to assist an innie child in adjusting to new routines, people, and experiences. The parts that follow will teach you how.

HELPING a young child deal with change

If they have to deal with a lot of changes all at once, young innies can go into meltdown. Minimising change is one of the best methods to assist a young innie in coping with it. Here are a few options for doing so:

- Create predictable habits to assist your child stay afloat in life's ever-changing tide. For example, if you have a toddler, try to keep her naps and mealtimes as constant as possible.
- Create consistent nighttime routines, such as a nightly story hour and back rub. If other aspects of her life become stressful or chaotic, she will be reassured by these routine activities.
- When changes do occur, do everything you can to

prepare your youngster. If you're divorced and your custody agreement changes, for example, inform your child right away about her new schedule. Create a calendar for her if she's old enough so she can see when she'll be at your house or your ex's.

TEACHING AN OLDER child or teen to handle unpredictability

Older introverts can adapt to changes in their schedules, which is a useful talent to have because life doesn't always go according to plan! So teach your introverted child or teen some methods for adjusting to change effortlessly, such as the ones listed below.

Make the visualisation activities suitable for your youngster. If she's transitioning from primary to secondary school, for example, give her a quick tour of the school so she can get a sense of how it looks. Then have her imagine herself succeeding in other aspects of school, such as conversing pleasantly in the corridor with one new friend and then several new friends, scoring a goal on the football field, or giving a confident presentation in class.

TEACH YOUR CHILD how to overcome catastrophic thinking.

Ask your child questions like these if she is afraid about moving to a new town and says, "I'll never make new friends."

- Were you terrified when we first relocated to this place five years ago?
- Did you make any new friends while you were here?

- Do you think you'll like your new town and make friends there?

Concentrate on activities that can assist your child in overcoming pessimism and negative thinking.

Encourage your child to discover some "transferable" hobbies and activities to assist her in adjusting if she changes schools or communities (especially if you move frequently). A passion for computers or basketball, for example, can help your child adjust to a new circumstance and meet other kids who share similar interests.

Giving your innie her own private space

Introverted kids, especially when they're depressed, tend to retreat to a haven. So, if your child doesn't have her own room, give her a small area — perhaps a corner of the living room — to call her own. Please give her a comfortable chair and a table, and let her block off the rest of the world after she's settled in. (Alternatively, consider putting up a tent or a treehouse in your backyard.)

Also, if your innie establishes her own tiny refuge, respect her solitude.

Providing your child with private spaces will benefit both you and her. A grumpy introvert might extend her negativity to the rest of the family, and she'll pick up on your bad mood, making her even grumpier. You can break the loop by enabling her to "quarantine" herself when she wants some alone time.

Be mindful, too, that your innie may occasionally retreat to her personal area to manipulate your behaviour. For example, when her mother tells her off, the little girl with the wardrobe hideaway will sit there for hours to make her mother feel bad. If your introvert pulls the same stunt on you, remember that she enjoys being alone, so don't feel bad about leaving her alone until she's ready to rejoin the family.

Also, don't allow her to hide away from social or family

commitments. "Say something like, "You can stay in your room until 6:00, and then it's dinnertime."

Encouraging Friendships

It's easy for young extroverts to make friends — on the playground, in the classroom, on the football field, at parties — but it's not so easy for introverted kids. Fortunately, you can assist. In this part, let's see how you can help an innie child or teen make the few good friends she needs.

HELPING A YOUNGER child make friends

Young introverts, like adult introverts, aren't great at small conversation and don't quickly warm up to others. As an innie's parent, you'll have to put in a little extra effort to assist your cutie in making friends. Here are a few strategies that have shown to be effective:

- When your child is small, begin scheduling play dates. Set up one-on-one play dates rather than huge groups, and keep track of which children your child enjoys the most so you can invite them frequently. Plan activities that will naturally lead to conversations, such as cookie baking or video games.
- Look for activities in the neighbourhood that your child enjoys.
- Make events that capitalise on your child's interests and abilities. For example, if your child likes horses and is a good rider, see if she wants to take a few classmates for a horseback ride. She'll be more relaxed if she's in an environment where she's competent and confident.
- Create a signal that your child can use to alert you if she is feeling overwhelmed during a social

engagement. Step in when you spot that signal and give her an excuse to take a break. "Liz, could you go upstairs and see if your brother is still napping?" for example." Have her practice giving you this signal a few times to know how to use it when she wants a break from playing.
- Improve your child's social abilities. Ascertain that she understands how to share, take turns, say "please" and "thank you," and be a gracious mother. (Also, make sure she learns how to apologise if she misbehaves or hurts another child; apologising is a vital social skill that far too many parents overlook.) Use role-playing to help your child practice social skills.
- If your child is having trouble making friends, consider utilising a social script. You produce a script that concentrates on a specific social setting in this method. To help a young child prepare for a birthday celebration, for example, you can utilise a social script like this: *"On Saturday, I'm throwing a birthday celebration for myself. Four students will represent my class. They are going to bring me gifts. We're going to have cake. Everyone will sing "Happy Birthday" to me once I blow out the candles on the cake. After that, I'll open my gifts. When I unwrap each person's present, I will say "thank you." We'll all play for a while, and I'll show off my new toys to the other kids. My friends will then go home, leaving me alone to play with my toys."* For a week or so before an occasion, practice your social script every day. This way, your child will know what to expect on the big day and how to behave appropriately, which will improve his or her chances of making friends.

Afterword

In this "introvert positive" era, where introverts and their skills are increasingly accepted, we live in a once-in-a-lifetime opportunity to succeed in the workplace. Sure, cultural auto-fills will mean that not everyone will always understand us, but taking the effort to understand ourselves is an important first step. We understand that, while we may need to bend in a few respects to accommodate the current cultural predisposition toward extroversion, we do not need to break. We have valuable strengths as introverts that no one can take away from us, and we can use those strengths to excel in our careers. The world is blessed to have you here, and it can certainly benefit from your skills, insight, and introversion.

Feedback

Thank you for reading 'Why Being an Introvert is a Superpower'. We hope you enjoyed the book? If you have a free moment, please leave us some feedback on Amazon.

Also, scan the QR code below to visit our website where you can find more information on our range of books available.

 HackneyandJones.com

www.ingramcontent.com/pod-product-compliance
Lightning Source LLC
Chambersburg PA
CBHW031545080526
44588CB00018B/2703